Praise for *Jes*

"Lucid, compelling, and beautifu... ...courage women everywhere to t...
—Frank Viola, author of *God's F*... ...*and From Eternity to Here*

"For some time now, feminism and Christianity have been bedfellows, but primarily in the halls of academia. What Sarah Bessey does is claim the voice of feminism for her own Christian faith—an evangelical faith, no less! The result is a powerful and empowering narrative that both men and women will find compelling and readable."
—Tony Jones, theologian and author of *The New Christians*

"I love writers who are insightful enough to be cynical but choose not to be. I love books that help me see things I'd never noticed before—in life, in myself, in others, in the Bible, in Jesus. I love writing that makes reading enjoyable and easy, because I know how hard it is to write that way. For these reasons and more, I love *Jesus Feminist*. It's not 'just a woman's book.' In fact, it's the kind of book that will help both women and men see how unhelpful that distinction is."
—Brian D. McLaren, author, speaker, activist

"It's hard to navigate an extremely delicate and important issue with gentleness and intention. In *Jesus Feminist*, Sarah Bessey has clearly proven herself a master at the task. Bessey powerfully, yet gracefully, compels both genders to rethink the role and value of women in the Christian faith, and emboldens women to know and live out that intrinsic value within the Body of Christ. *Jesus Feminist* is a critically important work; a must-read for everyone in the Church."
—Nish Weiseth, author of *Speak: How Your Story Can Change the World*

"Sarah says she doesn't feel a call to preach, but she speaks with the fire and artistry of a great preacher. Her sermon is one of hope: though the Church has often ignored the voices of women or lumped them into one limiting category, a revolution is coming. Sarah's voice is prophetic and she will free other women to speak and act with power, love, and courage. And may it be a summons for men in the Church to speak less and listen a lot more."

—Adam S. McHugh, author of *Introverts in the Church*

"With grace, humility, and confidence (even in the unknown), Sarah Bessey's *Jesus Feminist* masterfully humanizes one of the most controversial topics of the day. Bessey realizes that life, love, and faith cannot happen without community and the understanding that 'controversy' is less about sides and more about being whole together."

—Andrew Marin, author of *Love Is an Orientation*

"If you never imagined yourself as a card-carrying Jesus Feminist, this book will give you second thoughts. Sarah Bessey makes her case—not as a fire-breathing debater—but as a woman utterly captivated by Jesus who will stop at nothing to follow him. Her winsome writing made me laugh, cry, and stand taller as a woman. Unless I'm mistaken, it should swell the ranks of Jesus Feminists too. Sign me up!"

—Carolyn Custis James, author of *Half the Church: Recapturing God's Global Vision for Women*

"Sarah Bessey is so gifted a writer, so smart and welcoming and humble, the Church might not even notice how often it gets kicked between its 'doctrinally sound traditions,' where it hurts. But what makes *Jesus Feminist* so fantastic, so challenging, is Bessey's ability to be both the friend who tells us the truth about womanhood inside our churches and the sage who shows us how Jesus embraced equality and how we can do it better. With *Jesus Feminist*, Bessey is a modern-day Moses, seeking to not only free a Church held captive by dogma but also to redeem generations of women who have been stifled and silenced far too long."

—Matthew Paul Turner, author of *Churched*

"*Jesus Feminist* is a book that needed to be written! With honest vulnerability and a strong biblical foundation, Sarah Bessey shares her very personal journey and insight regarding the roles and qualifications for women in ministry. This book is a call and an invitation toward freedom and accountability. With honor and high regard for men and women alike, it beautifully portrays the wonder of what can happen when we take our places together and walk out the gifts and callings that God has placed within us as His Church."

—Helen Burns, author of *The Miracle in a Mother's Hug* and *What Dads Need to Know about Daughters/What Moms Need to Know about Sons*

"I want to write like Sarah Bessey. What she does with words is extraordinary, and the topic she's chosen is so deeply important. *Jesus Feminist* is a beautiful, challenging, rich, gutsy book, an absolute must-read."

—Shauna Niequist, author of *Bread & Wine*

"I've read countless books addressing the place of women in the kingdom, and I have never, ever read anything so lovely, so generous, profound, and humble as *Jesus Feminist*. If you're expecting anger or defensiveness or aggression, move on. If you are looking for intelligence and warmth and spirit, read this immediately. Regardless of where you enter this discussion, Sarah has created an astonishingly safe place to gather, discuss, process, and celebrate as women dearly loved by Jesus and created for his glory."

—Jen Hatmaker, author of *7: An Experimental Mutiny Against Excess* and *Interrupted: Relearning the Adventures of Faith*

EXPLORING GOD'S RADICAL NOTION
THAT WOMEN ARE PEOPLE, TOO

JESUS
FEMINIST

AN INVITATION TO REVISIT THE BIBLE'S VIEW OF WOMEN

SARAH BESSEY

HOWARD BOOKS
A Division of Simon & Schuster, Inc.
New York   Nashville   London   Toronto   Sydney   New Delhi

Howard Books
A Division of Simon & Schuster, Inc.
1230 Avenue of the Americas
New York, NY 10020

First Howard Books trade paperback edition November 2013

HOWARD and colophon are trademarks of Simon & Schuster, Inc.

For information about special discounts for bulk purchases,
please contact Simon & Schuster Special Sales at 1-866-506-1949
or business@simonandschuster.com.

The Simon & Schuster Speakers Bureau can bring authors to your live event. For
more information or to book an event contact the Simon & Schuster Speakers
Bureau at 1-866-248-3049 or visit our website at www.simonspeakers.com.

Designed by Davina Mock-Maniscalco

Manufactured in the United States of America

20   19   18   17   16   15   14   13   12

Library of Congress Cataloging-in-Publication Data

Bessey, Sarah.
   Jesus feminist / Sarah Bessey.
       pages cm
Includes bibliographical references.
   1. Women in Christianity. 2. Sex role—Religious aspects—Christianity.
   3. Feminist theology. I. Title.
       BV639.W7B46 2013
       230.082—dc23
                                                        2013015282

ISBN 978-1-4767-1725-8
ISBN 978-1-4767-1757-9 (ebook)

For Brian
MTB

Contents

FOREWORD   xiii

Let Us Be Women Who Love   xvii

INTRODUCTION: A Bonfire on the Shore   1

CHAPTER ONE: Jesus Made a Feminist Out of Me   11

CHAPTER TWO: A Redemptive Movement   25

CHAPTER THREE: Tangled-Up Roots   33

CHAPTER FOUR: The Silent(?) Women of Paul   55

CONTENTS

CHAPTER FIVE: Dancing Warriors   71

CHAPTER SIX: Patron Saints, Spiritual Midwives,
and "Biblical" Womanhood   87

CHAPTER SEVEN: A Narrative Reborn   105

CHAPTER EIGHT: Reclaiming the Church Ladies   123

CHAPTER NINE: Moving Mountains One Stone
at a Time   139

CHAPTER TEN: Kingdom Come   159

CHAPTER ELEVEN: Intimate Insurgency   177

CHAPTER TWELVE: The Commissioning   191

A Few Notes   199

Thank You   203

Discussion Questions   207

Further Reading   213

Notes   217

Foreword

Poet Maya Angelou said, "There is no agony like bearing an untold story inside of you." For women who bear the stories of patriarchy, freedom begins with the telling; it begins with those first tender words spoken out loud or written down on paper: "When I was a little girl," "I remember," "Once."

I listen as these stories emerge around many shared tables, with dinner rolls and wine between us, the butter softening and the candles dripping as we talk into the night. A young seminarian shares the disappointment of speaking to an empty room the day she gave her first sermon in preaching class and none of her male classmates showed up. A pastor recounts the time she approached a lectern at a conference, only to see a man in the second row turn his chair around so he wouldn't have to face her. A funny, animated girl describes the relief she felt when she and her husband of ten years realized they could function as a team of equal partners, instead of imposing ill-fitting, hierarchal gender roles onto their relationship. A young mother quietly recounts the sexual abuse she suffered in the name of "biblical submission."

I tell the story of standing before my high school youth group to give my first public testimony. Just sixteen, I breathlessly made my way through the familiar tale—lost to found, blindness to sight, wretch to born again. When I finished, I sat down next to a classmate, who turned to me and said, "You're a really good preacher, Rachel. *Too bad you're a girl.*"

These stories are followed by groans, by laughter, by tears, by commiseration, by celebration, and often by sacred silence. They are being told in living rooms, sanctuaries, Sunday school classrooms, coffee shops, campsites, rural villages, city streets, and chat rooms all around the world. In the company of one another, women are finding their voices, telling untold stories, and singing freedom songs. A movement is underfoot, a holy rumbling. And things will never be the same.

In this movement of stay-at-home moms and biblical scholars, CEOs and refugees, artists and activists, Sarah Bessey has quickly become one of my favorite storytellers. I have followed her for several years now, and what I love most about her work is the quiet strength with which she goes about it, the way in which she proves you don't have to speak in anger to speak a hard truth. I think of Sarah as a big sister in the faith, a woman whose wisdom and maturity challenge me, but whose honesty and vulnerability remind me that she's walking by my side in this journey, one arm over my shoulder.

On her blog, and in this wonderful book, Sarah does what all good storytellers do: she gives us permission—permission to laugh, permission to question, permission to slow down a bit, permission to listen, permission to confront our fears, permission to share our own stories with more bravery and love. As she puts it, "There is more room! There is more room! There is room for all of us!"

One word at a time, Sarah liberates us from the agony of bearing our stories alone, so we can follow Jesus (my favorite feminist) with more freedom and joy. I am so grateful.

Rachel Held Evans, author of *Evolving in Monkey Town*
and *A Year of Biblical Womanhood*
rachelheldevans.com

Let Us Be Women Who Love[1]

Idelette McVicker

Let us be women who Love.
Let us be women willing to lay down our sword words, our
sharp looks, our ignorant silence and towering stance and
fill the earth now with extravagant Love.
Let us be women who Love.
Let us be women who make room.
Let us be women who open our arms and invite others into an
honest, spacious, glorious embrace.

Let us be women who carry each other.
Let us be women who give from what we have.
Let us be women who leap to do the difficult things, the
unexpected things and the necessary things.
Let us be women who live for Peace.
Let us be women who breathe Hope.
Let us be women who create beauty.
Let us be women who Love.

Let us be a sanctuary where God may dwell.
Let us be a garden for tender souls.
Let us be a table where others may feast on the goodness of God.
Let us be a womb for Life to grow.
Let us be women who Love.

Let us rise to the questions of our time.
Let us speak to the injustices in our world.
Let us move the mountains of fear and intimidation.
Let us shout down the walls that separate and divide.
Let us fill the earth with the fragrance of Love.
Let us be women who Love.

Let us listen for those who have been silenced.
Let us honour those who have been devalued.
Let us say, Enough! with abuse, abandonment, diminishing
    and hiding.
Let us not rest until every person is free and equal.
Let us be women who Love.

Let us be women who are savvy, smart, and wise.
Let us be women who shine with the light of God in us.
Let us be women who take courage and sing the song in our
    hearts.
Let us be women who say, Yes to the beautiful, unique
    purpose seeded in our souls.
Let us be women who call out the song in another's heart.
Let us be women who teach our children to do the same.
Let us be women who Love.

Let us be women who Love, in spite of fear.

Let us be women who Love, in spite of our stories.

Let us be women who Love loudly, beautifully, Divinely.

Let us be women who Love.

A Bonfire on the Shore

Here, let's do this. Let's try to lay down our ideas, our neatly organized Bible verses, our carefully crafted arguments. Let's take a break from sitting across from each other in this stuffy room.

Let's head outside. I want us to sit around a fire pit ringed with stones and watch the moon move over the Pacific. I want us to drink good red wine, dig our toes into the cool sand, and wrap up in cozy sweaters. We'll feel the cold of the evening steal across the water soon, and the mountains are resting with their hands folded.

And I want us to talk about this—really talk about womanhood, church, the labels, and where we go from here. Because the vicious arguments, the limits, the you're-in-but-they're-out, the debates, and the silencing aren't working, are they? We have often treated our communities like a minefield, acted like theology is a war, we are the wounded, and we are the wounding.

I'll be honest: some of the words I have to say might rub you wrong. You might disagree with particulars, but that's okay—stay with me. Let's sit here in hard truth and easy beauty, in the tensions of the Now and the Not Yet of the Kingdom of God, and let us discover how we can disagree beautifully.

No matter the "side" or doctrine, experiences or tradition behind you, I know that you come bearing wounds. Don't we all? Perhaps someone has explained away your gifts and your callings, your abilities and your wisdom—maybe even your marriage, your stories, your testimony. Someone may have clobbered you with paragraphs and words and proof texts, made you feel like you are wrong somehow, either in your practice or your orthodoxy or your very created and called self. Perhaps they have hurt you, stifled you, broken you, bound you, held you, and cornered, abused, badgered, limited, and silenced you or someone you love. I know; yes, I know. And perhaps you have committed these very same sins against another soul.

Here, luv. Take a moment to refill your glass, and we can toast the truth with a bit of bitterness in our smiles. It's okay; I understand. I brought a thermos of strong tea, too, for later.

You know us Canadians—we love our tea (it's hard to be overly tragic while drinking tea).

I've got a crazy idea for you.

Let's be done lobbying for a seat at the Table. You know—that fabled "Table" we all talk about: "We just want a seat at the Table!" we say.

I've got a crazy idea for you. Let's be done lobbying for a seat at The Table.

It's the Table where all the decisions are made. Gatekeepers surround it, all reading the same books, spouting the same talking points, quoting each other back and forth, vilifying or mocking their straw men and women. It's the Table where coalitions and councils metaphorically sit in swivel chairs to discuss who is *in* and who is *out*, who is right (usually each other) and who is wrong (everyone else), and the perennial topic of whether women should be allowed to teach or preach or even read Scripture aloud. We've heard a lot about how men and women should think or act or look, how marriages should look, how children should be raised; and there's a good amount of social arguing, divisive labeling, name-calling, and even a bit of consigning-to-hell.

All too often, we abdicate our souls to these gatekeeper edicts. We're a bit too quick to choose a new shepherd instead of the rabbi from Nazareth, and we're all like ancient Israel, longing for a "real" king we can see and follow.

Look at this sky above us. Look up and see God's first cathedral. May you rest in your place in the story of God for a while and slow your urgent scrabbling breath here tonight. It didn't begin with us; it won't end with us, and who wants to live in an ivory tower when there is fresh air to breathe anyway?

I want to be outside with the misfits, with the rebels, the dreamers, second-chance givers, the radical grace lavishers, the ones with arms wide open, the courageously vulnerable, and among even—or maybe especially—the ones rejected by the Table as not worthy enough or right enough.

The Table may be loud and dominant, but love and freedom are spreading like yeast. I see hope creeping in, destabilizing old power structures. I feel it in the ground under my feet. I hear it in the stories of the people of God living right now. We're whispering to each other, eyes alight, "Aslan is on the move." Can't you feel that? The kingdom is breathing among us already.

I want to stand outside here in our Canadian wilds beside the water, banging my battered old pots and pans into the wind and the cold and the heavens, hollering, "There is more room! There is more room! There is room for all of us!"

We are among the disciples who are simply going outside, to freedom, together, intent on following Jesus; we love him so. We're finding each other out here, and it's beautiful and crazy and churchy and holy. We are simply getting on with it, with the work of justice and mercy, the glorious labor of reconciliation and redemption, the mess of friendship and community, the guts of walking on the water, and the big-sky dreaming of the Kingdom of God.

So may there be grace and kindness, gentleness and love in our hearts, especially for the ones who we believe are profoundly wrong. The Good News is proclaimed when we love each other. I pray for unity beyond conformity, because loving-kindness preaches the gospel more beautifully and truthfully than any satirical blog post or point-by-point dismantling of another disciple's reputation and teaching. I don't worry about the Table much anymore. Let's pray for them, forgive them where they have hurt us, and pray for those wounded in our collective cross fire. Let's be gentle in our dealings with them, but then let's get on with it.

A quiet shift has happened in my heart as I see and live and work and love with our sisters and brothers all over the world. It's a shift toward hope and grace, toward freedom over fear, life over death.

Years ago, I practiced anger and cynicism, like a pianist practices scales, over and over. I *practiced* being defensive—about my choices and my mothering, my theology and my politics. And then I went on the offense. I repeated outrage and anger. I jumped, Pavlovian, to right every wrong and defend every truth, refute every inflammatory blog post, pontificate about every question. Any sniff of disagreement was a dinner bell clanging to my anger: *Come and get it! Rally the troops!* Like many of us, I

Years ago, I practiced anger and cynicism, like a pianist practices scales, over and over.

5

called it critical thinking to hide my bitter and critical heart, and I wondered why I had no real joy in this ongoing search for truth.

Then, I wanted to be done with that grand piano performance of my own greatness and righteous anger, along with the glossy stage. So much for the concert proficiency at being right; I'm ready to be Beloved instead. Out here, on this same shore, those years ago, I imagined that I found a battered, old thrift-store piano. As I saw it, I was clumsy and awkward, learning to practice goodness and truth, like scales all over again. I am still practicing gentleness and beauty, over and over again. Someday perhaps my fingers will find those keys without thought.

I want to practice faithfulness and kindness; I am learning to fill my ears with the repetitions of wide eyes and open hands and innocent fun, holy laughter. I want to practice with intention, joy. I want to tell the truth, but first, I want to live the Truth.

I won't desecrate beauty with cynicism anymore. I won't confuse critical thinking with a critical spirit, and I will practice, painfully, over and over, patience and peace until my gentle answers turn away even my own wrath. I will breathe fresh air while I learn, all over again, grace freely given and wisdom honored; and when my fingers fumble, when I sound flat or sharp, I will simply try again.

We'll practice the ways of Jesus, over and over, until the scales fall from our eyes and our ears begin to hear. And someday, I believe, our fingers will be flying over the keys of that old piano, in old hymns and new songs, and when we look up, I bet there will be a field full of people dancing, beside the water, whirling, stomping their feet and laughing, and babies will be bouncing, and we will be singing the song we were always and ever meant to sing. The rocks will be crying out, and the trees will be clapping their hands, and the banquet table will be groaning with the weight of apples and wine and bread, and we will all sing until the stars come down.

Maybe it's not as sexy to tell the good, hopeful stories, all of the ways the Bride grows more beautiful to our eyes as she ages. It's not as fun as challenging the status quo or thundering down judgments on everyone else's way. The revolution of love takes many different forms, most of them good and courageous for their very differences. And I remain thankful for the people called to the hard work of pragmatics and iron-sharpening-iron conflict. Sometimes we turn over tables in the temple, and other times, we invite conversation by starting with an apology. This is just one fire on the shore; I see others around us, but I like my spot.

I could spend my life telling the beautiful stories of ordinary radicals, of the normal people sitting right beside you in that wooden pew and in the movie theater–style seat at the megachurch, the living rooms and the back alleys, the refugee camps and kitchen tables, and I would still run out of time because there are so many pockets of love and freedom in the church.

This night, by this bonfire, I want to wrap us up in the warmth of good stories, of strong love, prophetic callings. We'll wrestle with the deep biblical truth, tell a few everyday-hero stories of regular people just like you and me, down through the ages, whispered and shouted in the truth of freedom found, and our love of a Church whose only goodness is found in Christ alone, walking in the unforced rhythm of living loved by God. To me, our time together here is really about setting up our outposts of the Kingdom of God right in the teeth of the lies of the enemy.

And someday—I really believe this—we will throw our arms around the people of the Table as they break up the burnished oak. We'll be there to help them heave it out the windows, smashing every glass ceiling: the transparent, mirrored, and stained glass—all shards of broken lies now. We'll stand before the piles of stones that used to be weapons, and we'll build an altar. God met us here. We'll light another bonfire with the broken wood and splinters from the Table, and then we'll dance around those old arguments together, laughing.

So here's my own small offering for you. I'm determined to share it, to pour it out unfinished, imperfect. Leonard Cohen writes that there is a crack in everything—that's how the light gets in.[1] And hallelujah, I also think it's how the light gets out.

Perhaps it is no wonder that the women were first at the Cradle and last at the Cross. They had never known a man like this Man—there never has been another. A prophet and teacher who never nagged at them, never flattered or coaxed or patronized; who never made arch jokes about them, never treated them as "The women, God help us!" or "The ladies, God bless them!"; who rebuked without querulousness and praised without condescension; who took their questions and arguments seriously; who never mapped out their sphere for them, never urged them to be feminine or jeered at them for being female; who had no axe to grind and no uneasy male dignity to defend; who took them as he found them and was completely unselfconscious. There is no act, no sermon, no parable in the whole Gospel that borrows its pungency from female perversity; nobody could guess from the words and deeds of Jesus that there was anything "funny" about woman's nature.

Dorothy Sayers, *Are Women Human?*

CHAPTER ONE

Jesus Made a Feminist Out of Me

Jesus made a feminist out of me.

It's true.

I can't make apologies for it, even though I know that *Jesus* plus *feminist* might be the one label that could alienate almost everyone. I understand that—I do.

I know feminism carries a lot of baggage, particularly within the evangelical church. There are the stereotypes: shrill killjoys, man-haters, and rabid abortion-pushers, extreme lesbians, terrifying some of us on cable news programs, deriding motherhood and homemaking. Feminism has been blamed for the breakdown of the nuclear family, day care, physical and sexual abuse, hurricanes, the downfall of "real manhood," the decline of the Christian Church in Western society, and spectacularly bad television. Most of what has passed for a description of feminism is fearmongering misinformation.

In some circles, using the word *feminist* is the equivalent of an f-bomb dropped in church—outrageous, offensive. It's likely some people saw this book sitting on the shelf and figured they knew what sort of author was behind the words written here: a bitter man-hater arguing that men and women had no discernable differences, a ferocious and humorless woman, perhaps, and so it's no wonder they reacted at the sight of *Jesus* alongside *feminist* like someone had raked long fingernails across a chalkboard. Who could blame them with the lines we've been fed about feminists for so long?

It's a risk to use the word *feminism* here in this book—I know. But it's a risk I'd like you to take with me. Me? I like the word *feminist*, even if it worries people or causes a bit of pearl clutching. The word *feminist* does not frighten or offend me: in fact, I'd like to see the Church (re)claim it.

Some people think the concept of a Christian feminist is a misnomer, an embarrassing and misguided capitulation to our secular culture. It might surprise antifeminists and anti-Christians equally to know that feminism's roots are tangled up with the strong Christian women's commitments to the temperance movement, suffragist movements, and in America and England in particular, the abolitionist movements of the nineteenth century.[1] There is a rich tradition of pro-life feminism, which continues today.[2] Christian feminism predates the works of second- and third-wave secular feminist writers, such as Betty Friedan, Simone de Beauvoir, Gloria Steinem, Rebecca Walker, and Naomi Wolf. Feminism is complicated and it varies for each person, much like Christianity. It's not necessary to subscribe to all the diverse—and contrary—opinions within feminism to call oneself a feminist.

Feminism gained popularity as a result of "secular" work and scholarship, but the line between sacred and secular is man-made. Because God is the source of truth, Christians can still give thanks to God for the good works associated with feminism, such as the gaining of status for women as "persons" under the law, voting, owning property, and defending them-selves in a court of law against domestic violence and rape. As Canadian theologian Dr. John G. Stackhouse Jr. says, "Christian feminists can celebrate any sort of feminism that brings more justice and human flourishing to the world, no matter who is bringing it, since we recognize the hand of God in all that is good."[3] Modern Christian feminism is alive and well, from social justice movements to seminaries and churches to suburban living rooms, worldwide.

At the core, feminism simply consists of the radical notion that women are people, too. Feminism only means we champion the dignity, rights, responsibilities, and glories of women as equal in impor-

At the core, feminism simply consists of the radical notion that women are people, too.

tance—not greater than, but certainly not less than—to those of men, and we refuse discrimination against women.[4]

Several years ago, when I began to refer to myself as a feminist, a few Christians raised their eyebrows and asked, "What *kind* of feminist exactly?" Off the top of my head, I laughed and said, "Oh, a Jesus feminist!" It stuck, in a cheeky sort of way, and now I call myself a Jesus feminist because to me, the qualifier means I am a feminist precisely *because* of my lifelong commitment to Jesus and his Way.

PATRIARCHY IS NOT God's dream for humanity.

I'll say that again, louder, and I'll stand up beside our small bonfire and shout it out loud. I'll scare the starfish and the powerful alike: patriarchy is not God's dream for humanity. It never was; it never will be.

Instead, in Christ, and because of Christ, we are invited to *participate* in the Kingdom of God through redemptive movement—for both men and women—toward equality and freedom. We can choose to move with God, further into justice and wholeness, or we can choose to prop up the world's dead systems, baptizing injustice and power in sacred language. Feminism is just one way to participate in this redemptive movement.

In the context of our conversation here, two common labels used regarding the roles and voices of women in the church today, for better or for worse, are *egalitarian* and *complementarian*.

In general, according to theologian Carolyn Custis James, egalitarians "believe that leadership is not determined by gender but by the gifting and calling of the Holy Spirit, and that God calls all believers to submit to one another." In contrast, complementarians "believe the Bible establishes male authority over women, making male leadership the biblical standard."[5]

Both sides can treat the Bible like a weapon. On both sides, there are extremists and dogmatists. We attempt to outdo each other with proof texts and apologetics, and I've heard it said that there is no more hateful person than a Christian who thinks you've got your theology wrong. In our hunger to be right, we memorize arguments, ready to spit them out at a moment's notice. Sadly, we reduce each other, brothers and sisters, to straw men arguments, and brand each other "enemies of the gospel."

I know some people like to poke holes in each other's arguments, pointing out inconsistencies and trading jabs of verses and scholars and church history like scrappy boxers. Some do this well, with kind skill and mutual respect, and it's a joy to behold as they learn from each other. Others seem a bit more like mud wrestlers, hanging out on blogs or Facebook comment sections, at boardroom tables or in classrooms, at coffee shops or Christian bookstore shelves, with a lot of outrage—all in an effort to figure out how the other guy is wrong; it's theology as a fight-to-the-death competition.

And all God's people said, "That's exhausting."

So could we agree on one quick thing before I keep going? I think the family of God is big and diverse, beautiful and global. So these dogmatic labels, while sometimes useful for discussion in books and classes, aren't always the right boundaries for a life or a relationship. Most of us live somewhere in the in-between.

Let's agree, for just a little while anyway, that both sides are probably wrong and right in some ways. I'm probably wrong, you're probably wrong, and the opposite is true, because we still see through a glass, darkly.[6] I want to approach the mysteries of God and the unique experiences of humanity with wonder and humility and a listener's heart.

I have tried to stop caring about the big dustups between complementarians and egalitarians. I'm pretty sure my purpose here on earth isn't to win arguments or perform hermeneutical gymnastics to impress the wealthiest 2 percent of the world. I don't think God is glorified by tightly crafted arguments wielded as weaponry. Besides, I highly doubt this one slim book by a happy-clappy starry-eyed Jesus-loving Canadian mama will put any of this debate to bed when so many scholars and smarter-than-me people continue to debate and argue. That's not what I'm after.

After years of reading the Gospels and the full canon of Scripture,

> After years of reading the Gospels and the full canon of Scripture, here is, very simply, what I learned about Jesus and the ladies: he loves us.

here is, very simply, what I learned about Jesus and the ladies: he loves us.

He loves us. On our own terms. He treats us as equals to the men around him; he listens; he does not belittle; he honors us; he challenges us; he teaches us; he includes us—calls us all beloved. Gloriously, this flies in the face of the cultural expectations of his time—and even our own time. Scholar David Joel Hamilton calls Jesus' words and actions toward women "controversial, provocative, even revolutionary."[7]

Jesus loves us.

In a time when women were almost silent or invisible in literature, Scripture affirms and celebrates women. Women were a part of Jesus' teaching, part of his life. Women were there for all of it.

Mary, the mother of God, was a teenage girl in an occupied land when she became pregnant with the Prince of Peace, and as Rachel Held Evans points out, Scripture emphasizes that her worthiness is in her obedience "not to a man, not to a culture, not even to a cause or a religion, but to the creative work of a God who lifts up the humble and fills the hungry with good things."[8]

Even Mary's Magnificat is surprisingly subversive and bold, isn't it?[9] In the face of evidence to the contrary, she sings how she is blessed, how God lifts up the lowly, filling the hungry with good things and sending the rich away empty.

Throughout the records of the Gospels, I saw how Jesus didn't treat women any differently than men, and I liked that.

We weren't too precious for words, dainty like fine china. We received no free pass or delicate worries about our ability to understand or contribute or work. Women were not too sweet or weak for the conviction of the Holy Spirit, or too manipulative and prone to jealousy, insecurity, and deception to push back the kingdom of darkness. Jesus did not patronize, and he did not condescend.

Just like men, women need redemption. We all need the Cross of Jesus Christ, and we all need to follow him in the Way of life everlasting. In the words and actions of Christ as recorded in Scripture, we see what "neither male nor female, Jew nor Greek, slave nor free" looks like in real, walking-around life.[10]

During his time on earth, Jesus subverted the social norms dictating how a rabbi spoke to women, to the rich, the powerful, the housewife, the mother-in-law, the despised, the prostitute, the adulteress, the mentally ill and demon possessed, the poor. He spoke to women directly, instead of through their male-headship standards and contrary to the order of the day (and even of some religious sects today).

No, it was just him, incarnation of three-in-one on one. Women were not excluded or exempted from the community of God. Women stood before God on their own soul's feet, and he called us, gathered us, as his own.

When they threw the woman caught in adultery down into the dust at Jesus' feet and tried to use her shame to trap him, he leveled the playing field for both sin and marriage. There aren't too many of us women who don't imagine ourselves there, exposed, used, defiant or broken—sometimes both—and humiliated. And he, bless his name, restored, forgave, protected, drew a shield of grace around her with his dusty fingertip; and her accusers vanished. "Go," he said, "and sin no more."[11]

When the woman with the issue of blood reached out to touch the hem of his garment, Jesus did not respond with frustration. No, he touched her in return, praised her faith, set her free without recoiling."[12]

When Jesus healed the woman who was bent over, he did it in the synagogue, in full view. He called her "daughter of Abraham," which likely sent a shock wave through the room; it was the first time the phrase had ever been spoken.[13] People had only ever heard of "sons of Abraham"—never daughters. But at the sound of Jesus' words *daughter of Abraham*, he gave her a place to stand alongside the sons, especially the ones snarling with their sense of ownership and exclusivity over it all, watching. In him, you are part of the family; you always were part of the family.[14]

When Mary of Bethany sat at his feet, she was in the posture of a rabbinical pupil. Men and women rarely sat together, let alone for religious training, but there she was among them, at his feet. She was formally learning from him, the way the sons of Abraham had always sat—the daughters never had that spot. Even after Martha tried to remind her of her duties and responsibilities to their guests, Jesus defended her right to learn as his disciple; he honored her choice as the better one and said, "It will not be taken away from her."[15]

When Mary, the sister of Lazarus, reproached Jesus after her brother's death, he wept. In fact, he privately taught her one of the central tenets of our faith—the same thing he taught Peter: "I am the resurrection and the life"; this is the rock upon which he builds his church.[16] Martha received this teaching, too; she believed him, and where would we be if she hadn't shared what she heard from the lips of her beloved friend and Savior?[17]

When the Samaritan woman at the well met Jesus, he treated her like any other thirsty soul needing the living water.[18] She was leading a life that likely generated the hiss of shame and eyes of judgment. She was among the least valued and most dishonored of her day. Yet Jesus engaged her in serious theological discussion; in fact, hers is the longest personal conversation with Jesus ever recorded in Scripture. It was also the first time that the words "I am the Messiah" were spoken from his lips, and she became an evangelist. She told her story. She told of Jesus, and many were saved. When the disciples expressed their surprise at this turn, Jesus was matter-of-fact: this is simply the way of things.

When Jesus finished teaching in a synagogue one day, a woman called out from the audience, "God bless your mother—the womb from which you came, and the breasts that nursed you!" Yet Jesus replied to this common blessing with "But even more blessed are all who hear the word of God and put it into practice."[19] Women aren't simply or only blessed by giving birth to greatness; no, we are all blessed when we hear the Word of God—Jesus—and put it into practice. We don't rely on secondhand blessings in Jesus.

We also see seven women in the Gospels described with the Greek verb *diakoneo*, which means to minister or to serve. It's "the same one used to describe the ministry of the seven men appointed to leadership in the early church."[20] These women were Peter's mother-in-law; Mary Magdalene; Mary, the mother of Jesus and Joseph; Salome, the mother of Zebedee's sons; Joanna, the wife of Chuza; Susanna; and Martha, the sister of Mary and Lazarus.[21]

Even though the word of a woman was not considered sufficient proof in court, Mary Magdalene was the first witness of the resurrected Christ and the first preacher of the Resurrection. Jesus commanded her to go tell his brothers, the disciples, that he was returning to "my Father and your Father, to my God and your God." Before the male disciples even knew he was breathing, Jesus sent a woman to proclaim the good news: he is risen![22] The last shall be first, again, always.

> Even though the word of a woman was not considered sufficient proof in court, Mary Magdalene was the first witness of the resurrected Christ.

The women of the gospel narrative ministered to Jesus, and they ministered with him. The lack of women among the twelve disciples isn't prescriptive or a precedent for exclusion of women any more than the choice of twelve Jewish men excludes Gentile men from leadership.

We can miss the crazy beauty of it because of the lack of fanfare in Scripture. Women were simply there, part of the revolution of love, sometimes unnamed, sometimes in the background, sometimes the receiver, sometimes the giver—just like every other man in Scripture, to be engaged on their own merit in the midst of their own story.

Jesus thinks women are people, too.

The greatest issue facing the world today,
with all its heartbreaking needs, is whether those who,
by profession or culture, are identified as "Christian"
will become disciples—students, apprentices,
practioners—of Jesus Christ, steadily learning from him
how to live the life of the Kingdom of the Heavens
into every corner of human existence.

Dallas Willard, *The Great Omission*

CHAPTER TWO

A Redemptive Movement

Even now, after careful study and prayer, I don't imagine for a moment that I have the market cornered on truth or love. In fact, I've received a lot of wisdom, insight, teaching, friendship, and goodness from both egalitarians and complementarians across the spectrum on a variety of topics—including marriage and ministry, the prime points of disagreement between the two schools of thought.

No, my purpose in bringing you here tonight is actually to take a step out of those debates, to pursue a third way: a redemptive way. I want to turn our eyes from the thousands of arguments and the "he said, she said" of these fetishized camps in a small enclave of Western Christendom.

God has a global dream for his daughters and his sons, and it is bigger than our narrow interpretations or small box constructions of "biblical manhood and womanhood" or feminism; it's bigger than our frozen-in-time arguments or cultural biases, bigger than socioeconomics (or the lack thereof), bigger than marital status, bigger than our place, bigger than all of us—bigger than any one of us.

The beauty of this bigness is that it is small—down to each life. God's vision is a call to move forward into the future in the full operation of love, joy, peace, patience, kindness, goodness, gentleness, faithfulness, and self-control, with a fearlessness that could only come from him.

Wherever there is injustice or oppression, anything less than God's intended purposes from the dawn of Creation, our God has always set his people on the trajectory of *redemption*. The Cross is the center of this story—Christ and him crucified; the gospel is always glad tidings and great joy for all mankind. And now, we live and move in that truth and goodness; we live unveiled, and we are prophets and ambassadors of the God way of life.

God often works within human limitations or right-now situations to transform the world according to his good purposes. Plain English? God works with *whom* he's got and with what *we've* got—all to bring about his purposes.[1] Since Adam and Eve's sinful choices and the ongoing consequences, we have lived in this fallen world filled with suffering and pain and injustice; and even now, our world suffers under the weight and effects of patriarchy, too. Of course we ache for redemption: the whole of creation waits and groans with longing for the soon coming King.[2]

God longs to redeem the world; he longs to gather us like chicks to a mother hen. His passion for us is a father-mother sort of love; his loving-kindness will never fail; his desire is for our reconciliation to him. He cares about our place, about our lives, about the real physical and terribly beautiful earth.

And one way this is accomplished, generation by generation and in cooperation with free will, is through God's redemptive movement.[3]

Throughout Scripture, we see this redemptive movement of the Spirit in operation. Jesus often practiced the redemptive movement himself in the Gospels, showing how the Spirit moves the people of God (and therefore, eventually even humanity) further along toward his full intention. Jesus would teach or quote a portion of the Law and then *move us forward* from our current place toward God's original intent. For instance, instead of the familiar and accepted law of "an eye for an eye," Jesus moved the arc of redemption forward with, "But I tell you, love your enemies and pray for those who persecute

> Jesus would teach or quote a portion of the Law and then *move us forward* from our current place toward God's original intent.

you."[4] God is both here with us, and ahead, moving us onward to fullness.

An example of this redemptive movement in action during modern times is slavery. For centuries, the world at large was engaged in the practice of buying and selling other human beings as property. It was normal. Israel, and then the Church, participated in and even defended this heinous practice.

There are many verses in the Bible that discuss slavery in terms of logistics: Israel is held to a higher standard in its treatment of slaves (so that their humanity and rights are affirmed),[5] and in the New Testament, Paul encourages masters to treat their slaves fairly.[6] He encourages a master to welcome back a runaway slave to his household[7] and even advises slaves on how to best serve their masters.[8]

For hundreds of years, many Christians understood these references and instructions to imply that slavery was biblical and right.

Yet given God's creation and repeated prophetic mandates in Scripture of equality and freedom and justice for the oppressed, God's dream for humanity is clearly not slavery. The Church eventually moved to the forefront of abolition because it understood this truth: just because the Bible contained instructions about how to treat slaves in a context and culture where it was acceptable to hold slaves does not mean slavery is a godly practice or part of God's intended purpose for creation. As such, the Church has participated in God's trajectory of justice, living into the true purposes of God. Slavery and human trafficking are evil, and the Church must be part of God's plan to restore dignity and freedom to every human being. Even today, we continue to rescue those caught in the evil of slavery and human trafficking in our neighborhoods and internationally.

For instance, Christine and Nick Caine founded The A21 Campaign with the mission of abolishing injustice in the twenty-first century. Their work focuses primarily on freeing the twenty-seven million people enslaved in the world today. With individuals, churches, and government officials all in partnership, the organization focuses on human-trafficking prevention efforts, protection of victims through shelters and homes to help them move to stabilization, prosecution of perpetrators in the legal system, and intricate partnerships with local law enforcement, service providers, and communities.[9]

Take note, now. All this justice seeking, all this subversion, all this advocating and activism, all this battling to eradicate human trafficking happens despite the fact that there is actually *no specific verse in Scripture that prohibits the buying and selling of human beings*. Some verses even affirm proper treatment and behaviors of slaves.

And yet we accept and understand that slavery is evil precisely *because* of the Bible and because we understand God's created purpose for humanity. We hunger for justice for the oppressed precisely *because of* our deep love for God and our commitment to Scripture.

Sin entered the world, and with it came evil and injustices like slavery. God's redemptive movement for slaves began after the Fall with the proper treatment of slaves, and it has moved and stretched and bent toward the abolition movements worldwide in centuries past such as the Underground Railroad, and the modern-day abolition movements as exemplified by The A21 Campaign, among many other worthy organizations and individuals.

In addition to slavery, the Church has, in general, dismissed polygamy, the buying and selling of daughters, stonings, Levitical purity laws, the requirement of circumcision as the outward symbol of our covenant with God, and many other then-culturally-acceptable ancient practices.

God is still moving, still active, in our world today. The Church has been responding to the movement of the Spirit throughout the centuries, and gender inequality is only one more example of justice seeking in process. The Church has a rich and vibrant history of compassion and activism—and yes, over the years, many people have taken up the cause of women's rights worldwide, even the label of feminist, again, precisely *because of* their deep Christian faith.

As a Jesus feminist, I believe we are part of the trajectory of the redemption story for women.

As a Jesus feminist, I believe we are part of the trajectory of the redemption story for women in our churches, in our homes, in our marriages, in our parenting, in our friendships, and in our public lives. This trajectory impacts the story of humanity.

We are the people of God, and we are moving forward, always, prophetically embodying and moving toward God's *shalom*.

*Scratch any cynic
and you will find a disappointed idealist.*

George Carlin

CHAPTER THREE

Tangled-Up Roots

Let's pause for a moment. Pass the thermos, would you? Can anyone's story start with her own self? No, the story only includes us, and if we have any honesty at all, we must trace the line of time backward, meandering through memory and motivations before we move forward. Could you really hear any word from me without first knowing my story, without first knowing why I care, why any of this matters to me? My beginnings shaped who I am today. For me, I'll pick up the story with a small family in western Canada.

My parents were raised in early post-Christian homes. Their grandparents had been religious, but their parents were part of the generational shift that simply drifted away from church attendance and religious affiliation. They maintained a more-or-less connection to the values of their youth, but life got in the way: the wars, the work of keeping body and soul together. After all, the coal-mining towns of northern Alberta and the wheat fields and postwar cities of southern Saskatchewan don't give up a living easily; and then, of course, there was booze running through the story, through the blood, through the memories, sometimes a trickle, sometimes a torrent. My root people, my blood family, are gorgeous, deeply flawed, passionate, brilliant, funny-as-hell storytellers, and they are hard workers.

My dad grew up in Regina, his carrot-red hair an oft-repeated prophecy of his hot temper. He ran a bit crazy in his teen years, giving his mother fits. He was a son of the small town and the farm, the first generation to be raised in the city. My mother grew up stark thin and lonely, the fourth baby of a child bride from the coal towns of Alberta. There were a few bad years there in the middle of the growing up, those years on the Saskatchewan flats, but her family emerged from that fog to unnamed grace and began to scrabble their way to respectability, to mutual forgiveness and love.

My parents met outside their high school. My dad whisked her to a pub in the middle of the school day, and when she told him to take her back to school for her typing test, he grinned and said, "No way." They fell crazy in love, the way teenagers do, and in their wedding picture, they aren't standing sedately beside each other, beaming smug satisfaction about the nice life ahead. No, they are turned together, skinny hips squared, their arms locked tight around each other.

My mum and dad found Jesus spectacularly, in a turn-your-life-upside-down sort of way, during my childhood. When I was born, my mother felt inadequate, she didn't know if she had what it took to love me the whole way through life. She was barely twenty-three years old, wondering what love is, and where it comes from, and why we love and how. No answer felt like enough for her, especially when my sister arrived two years later. They had a happy little family in a red split-level in Regina, but still, the yearning for something *more* remained. Our teenage babysitter, Leila, went away to a Mennonite church camp one summer and came home "on fire for Jesus," as they said in those days. She looked around her small circle and knew we weren't Christians, so she bought a children's record for us, one called *Bullfrogs and Butterflies*.[1] My sister and I memorized all the catchy late seventies–style pop songs about how nothing compared to knowing God, not even riding bikes. But while we were at the elementary school across the back alley, my mother sat beside our little plastic record player, listening to the songs about bullfrogs and butterflies being born again, and she cried and cried and cried with longing, with an ache in her soul that said, "Yes, you were right, there is more—and *this is it.*"

She decided we should go to church, and so we all started

at a little Presbyterian church in town. But by now, my father's carefully hidden lifelong anxiety disorder had begun to take over his life. The smart-aleck young man with authority issues was twisted with stomach ulcers, a toxic mess of fear eating his life. One day, he heard the minister at church read something from the Bible about how Jesus healed people. He was still on the fence about the whole "God thing," but racked with the pain of anxiety and ulcers, he strode over in his cowboy boots and skinny jeans to ask that preacher if he really meant it.

My dad is a true Canadian kid, deeply distrustful of religion, Toronto, politicians, and the Establishment. He didn't like smells and bells, manipulations, or pleas for money. Any slobbering emotionalism sent him running. But the reverend said, yes—yes, God could and did heal. So my dad drove home and sat in our living room, and I guess you can call it praying, but he was talking more than praying, rather matter-of-fact. He said something along the lines of, "Well, Jesus, that preacher told me you can heal. If that's true, then I want you to heal me. I don't want ulcers, I don't want this anger, and I don't want anxiety and fear to run my life anymore. So if you could do that for me, well, then I'll know you're for real, won't I?"

And you can roll your cynical heard-it-all-before eyes at me, but the truth is this: he was healed. That night. In our living room. No formulas, no "right way" about it, no Bible verse quoting, not even that humble or contrite of a heart. Just a man, laying it out, like a hand of cards face up on the table, utterly done with playing. And God met him there, like a whirlwind, like the Great Physician, like a father, like a brother, like a friend, and utterly called his bluff.

When the Sunday school asked my mother to teach a class, she said, "Oh gracious, no—I'm not ready." So Mum came to Sunday school with me. She assisted the teacher, handed out crayons, set up small chairs. She simply wanted to learn about her Jesus.

I remember my Mum crying over her Bible, like it was a love letter.

I watched my dad get up early every single morning, without fail, and read his Bible like it was his lifeline. He wrote out his prayers from Scripture, longhand. When I couldn't sleep, my dad wrote beside my name that God gives sleep to his beloved.[2] When I was sick, he wrote beside my name that by Jesus' stripes I was healed.[3] When I dated men that made him scratch his head and petition heaven for strength, he wrote out that I was not to be unequally yoked.[4] (I wish I were kidding about that last one.)

I grew up at the kitchen table of grateful baby disciples with quickly worn-out Bibles and hungry hearts. We were without a tradition or reference point beyond our (apparently wrong) translation of the Bible, so we made our mistakes and we stumbled, and we memorized a lot of Bible verses. And when we struggled with despair and fear, with our own gross sins and failings, these sacred words and our never-ending conversations with our Savior and each other were our first stop. We were always expecting God's movement and divine answers and breakthrough miracles.

Whatever else went wrong in our lives—the sorrows of burying parents and friends, epic and still-present family rows and grudges, kids going off the rails, jobs lost, financial stress, rebellions, broken relationships, church politics, and failings— my parents were almost always steady. Now they are nearing the forty-years-married marker. It hasn't been perfect, but it's been good; it hasn't been easy, but it's been worth it. And God has been more than enough.

Here's the interesting thing to me now, through the prism of years, my own marriage and mothering, my reading, and the practice of church life: there was no sense of hierarchy, implied or otherwise, in our family. Over the years, my parents shared the responsibility for providing for our family and for the quotidian rhythms of meals, laundry, bills, and housework, which go into family life.

Then there was my church and community. We met in the school gym; our pews were folding chairs. We had an electric piano, maybe tambourines on a big day. We sang choruses, and I didn't learn a real hymn until my twenties. We spoke in tongues, shouted "Come on, preach!" during the sermon, and traded bootlegged teaching tapes from American preachers like trading cards. It wasn't perfect, and a lot of the theology was an over-realized eschatology bathed in nonaccredited Bible school education and literalism. But I loved it then and I love it still.

I grew up in a post-Christian community, usually one of just a few Christians in our public school mishmash, educated in a pluralistic understanding of religion and life. Most of my friends practiced a rather quiet form of humanism, a be-good-do-good, left-of-center working philosophy of morality. Mine was the generation raised by the first post-Christian generation of Canada; my friends' parents didn't bother anymore with church, even for Easter and Christmas, so my generation explores spirituality while abhorring the boundaries and exclusivity of most religions. We are distrustful of anyone preaching one way to do anything, from how to get to heaven on through to solving a math equation.

There weren't too many megachurches in my world. But we were starry-eyed children of the renewal movement, the third wave, without a real clue of our place in church history. We were a band of misfits, finding Jesus and being born again over and over. Our communities were smaller, more organic, more flat in hierarchy. We were there because we wanted to be there, not because anyone expected us to be there. The evangelical—and particularly the charismatic—Christian community here in western Canada is so intimate that we can play six degrees of separation in two degrees or less: we either know you or we know someone who knows you.

My dad and I have laughed over the Apostle Paul's opening in the first letter to the Corinthians: "Take a good look, friends, at who you were when you got called into this life. I don't see many of "the brightest and the best" among you, not many influential, not many from high-society families. Isn't it obvious that God deliberately chose men and women that the culture overlooks and exploits and abuses, chose these "nobodies" to expose the hollow pretensions of the "somebodies"? That makes it quite clear that none of you can get by with blowing your own horn before God. Everything that we have—right thinking and right living, a clean slate and a fresh start—comes from God by way of Jesus Christ."

That's us, all right.

And in every Sunday service I attended, there were women. Women prophesied with honor. They led key ministries. They preached. Taught. Read Scripture. Sang. Passed the clean plastic ice cream bucket serving as our official Tithe and Offerings plate. We sent women out as missionaries, single or married, far away from us, their smiling pictures tacked up to a corkboard in the foyer, a string of yarn connecting to pushpins of their locations on the map. I was completely comfortable with the title "Pastor" in front of a feminine name. The church ladies cooked and fed and danced with babies at the back of the room, sure, but they were also at the front. I grew up without knowing that anyone thought women could not or should not lead or preach or speak or follow the clear calling of God for their life. To us, it was not about your sex; it was about how God had gifted you. We didn't believe the gifts of the Spirit were sex-based.

We didn't believe the gifts of the Spirit were sex-based.

As Barbara Brown Taylor says, I knew all these things when I was young, but somehow, I forgot.[5]

My family then moved a few times, and we eventually landed in the young and thriving city of Calgary, Alberta. Now we were in a larger, well-established church with structure and rules. The church was energetic and optimistic, a mirror of the city itself, pulsing with Western opportunity and new money. Young people were often earmarked as "having a call for ministry" and then honored by the leadership. They were given responsibilities, mentoring opportunities, the microphone, a platform, and authority as their callings were affirmed and celebrated by the community.

But I noticed they were all boys. I had no desire to preach (I still don't), and I did not feel called to pastor or lead, so it wasn't exactly jealousy in my heart. But I had friends who did wish to preach or were called to local church ministry or to the mission field, perhaps. They were smart, ambitious, wise, gentle; they displayed all the telling characteristics of leadership as the church celebrated it.

Sometimes, these girls were affirmed as the future spouses of ministers or missionaries, the good women destined to be behind the great men. The leadership team boys all contemplated future wives from this pool of girls.

I was eighteen when I moved away from home. My parents and sister dropped me off in Oklahoma at a Christian liberal arts university, and they all cried the whole way home to Canada. Phone calls home cost more in those days, there was no Facebook, and e-mail was brand new and untried. I was fairly convinced one could perish of homesickness.

Eventually, I found my footing, and I found Jesus all over again as I began to learn about how big the family of God really is. I was dazzled by all of these Christians. *Everywhere! Christians! Churches! America is amazing!* I changed my major three times in an effort to figure out a way to be a writer and make a living at the same time without teaching high school English; and of course, Brian and I found each other. So much for my plan to travel through Europe after university before settling down and renting a studio in Montreal or New York while I "found my voice" as a writer. Instead I ran down a chapel aisle in my wedding dress toward a tall and steady Nebraskan with a ferocious work ethic. In our wedding picture, we look like a couple of kids headed off to prom.

We were terribly young, fresh faced, and married for only four months when we moved to Texas. I was at the beginning stages of a long season ahead: growing cynical, tired, questioning, doubting, disillusioned with church and the institutions of Christianity. I was deep into the familiar territory of second-generation Christians. Brian served a large-and-growing-larger evangelical church as a youth and college and career pastor, while I went to work in financial services marketing. I may have sourly told a few people, "This isn't a two-for-one deal" when they innocently asked what my role would be in his ministry.

The church had a history of egalitarianism. When the pastor died suddenly, his co-pastoring wife stepped in as lead pastor. Some in the conservative Texas town looked askance at Pastor Kathleen and her stylish blond hair, but she led the church for a few years, managing the staff of pastors and preaching weekly.[6] By the time we arrived, she had moved on to another church, so there were no longer any women pastors, and women held few key leadership positions. I believe it wasn't necessarily an intentional oversight or decision, as much as just the way things go sometimes.

A woman managed the children's ministry. Her role was almost identical to my husband's role as youth pastor: she preached, prepared sermons, organized programs, counseled, loved kids, trained leaders, attended strategy meetings, and managed a budget, among other staff duties such as prayer meetings and hospital visits. And yet the church called my husband Pastor Brian, and she was just Lisa. I couldn't figure out why her official title was director instead of pastor. I was told the omission of "Pastor" from her title was "for appearances"—to avoid a direct challenge to certain passages of Scripture about women being silent in the church, or "You know—how women can't be pastors." One person told me that it was also because if she had the title of pastor, she would automatically be part of the executive team, and the team needed to be only composed of men because a woman would change its dynamic. It was believed that her presence in their meetings would mean that the guys couldn't be as honest or open; she would upset the delicate accountability structure and honest dialogue of the inner sanctums of church leadership. Lisa did not let her lack of a title hold her back from building a complex and strong ministry centered on discipling kids in the ways of Jesus. Semantics and titles weren't her worry; she *pastored* those kids and their parents, whether anyone wanted to call her pastor or not.

Upon my introduction to the larger Church culture, I discovered that the way I grew up, particularly in terms of "women in ministry," was not common. Everywhere I turned, evangelical sermons on marriage were filled with "Oh, you know women" jokes. Generally speaking, women were perceived as soft, emotional, and naturally nurturing, while men were positioned as natural leaders, hating to talk about relationships, and requiring more sex. Male and female relationships were framed as fairy tales where women are encouraged to be passive receivers and men are the heroic rescuers or as a contest and exercise in combat and negotiation There was a lot of talk in those days of the "feminization of the Church" and how guys needed to step up and be men, which apparently resembled the ideal of benevolent dictators, rather than the Son of Man. I was genuinely baffled because when I looked at my husband, and even at my parents' marriage, this did not ring true. Since when did the "stepping up" of a real man require the bowing down or lessening of the woman he loves?

Women's ministry in those days primarily focused on married, stay-at-home mothers. I worked in a fast-paced financial industry alongside many other strong, well-educated, openly Christian women from a variety of traditions (this was Texas, after all)—leaders, influencers, financiers, decision makers—and not once were any of these women asked to help manage their own church's financial affairs or nominated as elders or deacons.

During this season of my life, the more I learned about Jesus, the more I struggled with the iterations of Christianity around me. Much of what I saw or experienced in the modern church didn't match up with what I thought I knew about the ageless God. My growing disenchantment was not limited to women's roles in the church, though: these "lady issues" were merely one branch in the thicket of my frustrations with the Church.

> The more I learned about Jesus, the more I struggled with the iterations of Christianity around me.

It started with the small questions, the easy ones to stuff into the closet and ignore. I could drown the questions and the cognitive dissonance out if I quoted enough Bible verses, if I went to enough church services, if I got busy "doing hard things for Jesus," made another casserole for another neighbor, led another youth retreat, hosted another Bible study, bought another leather-bound devotional with an unfurling flower on the cover, quieted down more, tried harder to fit into the getting-smaller-by-the-day understanding of following Jesus.

But my questions and doubts had the inconvenient habit of poking out the straining door, gathering friends, growing and intensifying as steadily as if my resolute denial of their existence fed and watered them.

I was drawn toward a life of redemptive peacemaking and justice seeking, yet the churches of my context and tradition were in a strange collusion with politics and just-war philosophy as the Iraq War began. I struggled with the cultural rhetoric against immigrants, homosexuals, artists, welfare recipients, the poor, non-Americans, and anyone who looked different or lived differently than the expectation. Cultural mores were passing as biblical mandates. The give-me-more-more-more prosperity gospel didn't match up with my growing commitment to contentment and simple living. I wanted my pro-life ethic to encompass all of human life.

For the first time in my life, I was reading and learning about the Church's mandate to care for the poor. I was reading voraciously about global issues such as clean water, community development, war, human trafficking, economics, disaster relief, the AIDS crisis, unjust systemic evils. Meanwhile, church budgets made room for a brand-new light show and a kickin' sound system or a trip to Disneyland or a video venue in a saturated upscale neighborhood—all in an effort to practice creative-experience marketing. And the rich got richer. The more I learned about the life and world and trage-dies thumping along beyond our seemingly missing-the-point building programs and Christian schools and drive-by mis-sionary work, the more I ached and grieved and repented of my own sin and blindness. I questioned it all, including my own commitment to propping up this system.

The cracks were ricocheting and multiplying across my heart now, and when I turned to the Church for answers, I did not feel my questions were welcome. This may have been my own pride and willful blindness, but there didn't seem to be room for me as a questioning woman within the system, as a seeker. I was straining to keep my barrage of questions stuffed in the closet. My stubborn faith was not lining up with the big, broad Church's priorities and focus. The whole women-can't-do-such-and-such or here's what-a-biblical/true/real-woman-does or submit-and-stay-home-and-have-babies subtext? Well, add that to the getting-bigger-by-the-day pile.

Do you remember the Saturday-morning cartoons where the bedroom closet was bulging with toys from a last-minute stuffing-in by the kids, and then the poor mum opens the door? And it all falls, pell-mell, tumble-bumble, onto her head. CRASH. Yes. Me, too. And that is exactly what happened with my crammed closet of doubts and questions and hurts.

Crash.

I know nothing for sure. Is God even real? What about my Bible? Church? People? Life? Meaning? Loss? Grief? Disillu-sionment? Soul weariness? Goodness? Evil? Tragedy? Suffering?

Justice? Women? Equality? Politics? I know nothing, nothing, nothing.

And it's not because I didn't have "answers"—oh, no. I had all of the photocopied apologetics cheat sheets lined up in a neatly labeled three-ring binder, paragraphs highlighted to respond to the questions of the ages, all in three lines or less. I clung tighter and tighter to their "answers," but the dry sand of my foundation was spilling out of my clenched fists, all the faster for the clinging.

We eventually left full-time, vocational ministry on good terms with blessings at our back, and we remain good, good friends with most of our church family there. The entire experience was a gift to me in every way—I see that now. I also have sincere regrets about the way I processed much of this shifting and changing; I've had to ask forgiveness from several friends and leaders. But the questions were legitimate, and now, I embarked on a journey through the wilderness of my wonderings with a seen-it-all-before smirk on my face and a profound ache in my soul.

But God set up a banquet in the wild places, streams of water flowed in the desert, and I walked and walked and walked right through the pain of disillusionment and despair, leaning into the wind.

We moved home to Canada. We abandoned our plans to church plant in this context, at least in the way we had been taught to do it in America. Instead, we embraced a new understanding of church and community, of vocation and ministry, of organic faith and missional living. We were lonely. And then we began to heal, slowly at first, then faster and faster.

"You can't be a Christian by yourself," writes Sara Miles.[7] Me? I tried.

I tried to be a Christian by myself. And in my deepest hurts from the Body of Christ, it did help to cocoon away in the in-between space for a while. It helped to step away from the institutions of church in a self-imposed blackout from the programs, from the self-perpetuating machine, from the politics, the religion, the expectations, the behavior modification, the CEO-style leadership courses, the unstable pedestals for pastors and the way that the grind of modern ministry life seems to chew up and spit out again, and the easy consumer spirituality.

The wilderness transformed me in a way that no "spiritual high" or certainty or mountaintop moment had ever done. I shed a lot of performance anxiety in those "in between" years. I reconciled what I believed and why. I embraced the glorious kaleidoscope of God at work in the global world. And most importantly, the wilderness was the birthplace of my intimacy with God. Jonathan Martin writes, "Far from being a punishment, judgment, or a curse, the wilderness is a gift. It's where we can experience the primal delight of being fully known and delighted in by God."[8]

I loosened my grip on my opinions. I entered recovery for being such a know-it-all. I stopped expecting everyone to experience God or church or life like I thought it should be done.

In fact, I stopped using the word *should* about God altogether, I sought God, and he was faithful to answer me. I came to know him as "Abba"—a Daddy. He set me free from crippling approval addiction, from my Evangelical Hero Complex, from the fear of man. He bathed my feet, bound my wounds, gave rest to my soul, restored the joy of church and community to our lives. I learned the difference between critical thinking and being just plain critical. And I found out that he is more than enough, always will be more than enough—yesterday, today, forever.

I learned the difference between critical thinking and being just plain critical.

Now, all these years later, I marvel. I marvel because God was there *in* the pain. I marvel because this life we lead back home in Canada is not what we would have imagined for our lives, but *it's so much better.* And I marvel because I hold almost all of it loosely in my hand now, all of it but this: the nature, identity, soul, action, and character of God is love— *lovelovelovelovelovelovelove.*

Everything was resurrected on that truth. And now for me, faith is less of a brick edifice of belief and doctrine and right answers than it is a wide-open sky ringed with pine trees black against a cold sunset, an altar, a welcome, bread and wine, an unfathomably ferocious love, and a profound sense of my belovedness.

It's tempting to make a rule out of my experience and tell you exactly what happened, my step-by-step redemption and reconciliation—as if because God worked this way for me, then surely he must work this way for you. But no. This birth of joy and goodness and restoration is mine alone, unique. You have yours—or you will have it, I believe.

While I was preparing for childbirth, I learned how much of the pain women experience during labor is related to our own fears and resistance to the pain. Dr. William Sears calls it the fear-tension-pain cycle.[9] Because we are afraid, we naturally hold back and tense up, and then there is more pain, so we experience even more fear, and on it goes, around and around, building with intensity on every turn. To interrupt the cycle, we need to surrender to what is happening, right now. We must lean *into* the pain instead of resisting it.

Each time I gave birth, it took everything in me to release the tension, to reject fear, to open myself up to what my body was doing. But when I did, I experienced the marked difference that leaning into the pain and sensations makes in delivery.

It seems counterintuitive; we should run from pain, right? But believe me: leaning into the pain makes giving birth easier.

I should be the mother of seven children, but there are only three tinies with us now. Believe this: I have learned to lean into some pain—to let the pain be there, part of me, without fear, without judgment, without refusal, because this is all part of the struggle of birth and life.

And the pain will, somehow, eventually, give way to blessed release and relief and, hopefully, joy.

I'll avoid the prescriptives and how-tos for both our sakes. Instead, if you are struggling to break that cycle of fear-tension-pain, I'll tell you a bit more about the God I love so wild but remember, the subtext for all of it is this truth: *lean into it*.

Lean into the pain.

Stay there in the questions, in the doubts, in the wonderings and loneliness, the tension of living in the Now and the Not Yet of the Kingdom of God, your wounds and hurts and aches, until you are satisfied that Abba is there too. You will not find your answers by ignoring the cry of your heart or by living a life of intellectual and spiritual dishonesty. Your fear will try to hold you back, your tension will increase, the pain will become intense, and it will be tempting to keep clinging tight to the old life; the cycle is true. So be gentle with yourself. Be gentle when you first release. Talk to people you trust. Pray. Lean into the pain. Stay there. And the release will come.

I know you have questions, and they're much bigger than the whole church-women-feminism-equality issues. I know. Me, too. Still. So I'll carry you in my heart. Stay as long as you'd like; I'm in no rush. Hurry wounds a questioning soul.

Hurry wounds a questioning soul.

My water in the desert arrived in cups fashioned by the hands of those who love the gospel. I found, right under my nose, people who love God and love others; their lives were a smelling-salts wake-up experience of grace. Sometimes they were the same people I lived alongside during those years of wondering and isolation in Texas. My loss is that, in my pride, I didn't see them there at the time. Everywhere I look now, I see disciples who forgive and serve without fanfare or book deals, working quietly for justice and mercy. They love the unlovable, the marginalized, the hopeless; they wash dishes and raise babies; they work in Surrey and in Port-au-Prince and San Antonio because of their great love for God. They believe Jesus actually meant all that stuff he spoke while here on earth, so they are on mission; they are peace*makers*.

Jesus said, "You must begin with your own life-giving lives. It's who you are, not what you say and do, that counts. Your true being brims over into true words and deeds."[10] You cannot be full to the brim with Christ's love and peace without spilling over into the lives of others. You learn how to love by being loved. You yearn to heal once you are healed. We receive goodness and bread, and then, of course, of course, we want to point every other hungry beggar on the road to the source.

In those days,
I will pour out my Spirit even on my servants—
men and women alike—and they will prophesy.

Acts 2:18

CHAPTER FOUR

The Silent(?) Women of Paul

The way of Christ is a narrow path. As we walk, we heart-wrestle, wondering; and we pray for wisdom and grace, courage, and company. When the well-meaning glibly parrot Bible verses, stomping through the thin places between the Spirit and my humanity with all the subtlety of a clumsy four-year-old boy, something in me needs a long, deep, cleansing breath—because these aren't just "issues" or "debates," are they? This very book, our conversation, this "issue" represents people with real lives and real stories and real hurts, real marriages and real churches and very real complex needs. The world is failing women, and we, the people of God, know the solution: our beloved Jesus and his Kingdom ways are good news, in every sense of the words.

Really, theology is simply what we think about God and then living that truth out in our right-now life.

To some, theology can seem a bit foreboding; to others, it's apparently a thrilling blood sport complete with cage matches between the big names. Really, theology is simply what we think about God and then living that truth out in our right-now life.

Of all the spiritual disciplines, reading my Bible has come easiest to me. I've always been a word girl—when I felt misunderstood as a teenager, my parents would find letters on their pillow explaining my positions in detail or an abject apology for an outburst. When that tall Midwestern boy dropped handwritten letters into my campus post office box throughout university, I tucked them into decorative shoe boxes, and then I married him.

The way to my heart has always been the written word. Now, after all of this time, all of this grappling love, I find when I write or speak, the words of Scripture are woven in, easily, unknowingly at times, like wine through water.

People want black-and-white answers, but Scripture is rainbow arch across a stormy sky. Our sacred book is not an indexed answer book or life manual; it is also a grand story, mystery, invitation, truth and wisdom, and a passionate love

letter. I've abandoned the idea that my job is to get the absolute, 100 percent right answers on everything. And my task
here, in this book, isn't to silence all discussion or find the
magic key that unlocks a "This is the answer! Case closed!
Court dismissed!" answer for you.

I *want* you to wrestle with the Bible. Do it. Wrestle until,
Jacob-like, you walk with a limp ever after, and you receive the
blessing of the Lord.[1]

So, can you be a Jesus feminist and still respect the Bible
for what it actually is instead of what you want it to be?[2] And
how can I advocate for welcoming the voices and experiences
of women in all levels of church and leadership when the
Bible clearly says women need to be silent and submissive in
church?

I've often heard the bumper-sticker phrase, "The Bible
says it, I believe it, that settles it." But that's not really true,
is it? Whether we admit it or not, as people of faith, we sift
our theology through Scripture, Church history and tradition,
our reason, and our own experience.[3] Most Christians, even
the most committed of the *sola scriptura* crowd, use these four
pillars—at varying degrees of importance and strength—to
figure out the ways of God in our world and what it means
here and now for our walking-around lives. And taking this a
bit further into postmodern territory, we can also admit that
we are relying on our own imperfect and subjective *interpretations* of those pillars, too.

I believe it's misguided, and probably profane, to look at a

diverse collection of books written over thousands of years—
history, poetry, law, Gospel accounts, proverbs, correspon-
dence, and other writings—as absolute literal instructions
without context, as we understand them, in all cases.

For instance, some evangelicals have turned Proverbs 31
into a woman's job description instead of what it actually is:
the blessing and affirmation of valor for the lives of women,
memorized by Jewish husbands for the purpose of honoring
their wives at the family table. It is meant as a celebration for
the everyday moments of valor for everyday women, not as an
impossible exhausting standard.[4]

We can miss the gospel forest for the word-by-word
trees. We try to make poetry and metaphor, history and letters fit into a prescriptive and literal box in all cases. We've
embarked on an adventure in missing the point, cloaking it
in "God said it!" smug sound-bite piety. We indulge in semantics and slippery-slope rhetoric to excuse injustice. We
read a few verses about women in a vacuum of literalism and
prideful laziness.

It's dangerous to cherry-pick a few stand-alone verses,
particularly when they are used as a weapon to silence and
intimidate, effectively benching half the church[5] in the midst
of holy harvest season when the harvest is plentiful and the
workers are few.[6]

But it is equally dangerous to simply get on with doing
what we "feel" is right. We cannot ignore any portions of
Scripture simply because they make our (post)modern selves

uncomfortable. We can't simply dismiss the parts of the Bible we don't like—not if we call ourselves followers of The (whole) Way. Nor should we weigh the desires or practices of our own culture and personal experiences to the exclusion of Scripture or tradition or reason. Theologian N. T. Wright believes that to affirm the "authority of Scripture" is precisely "not to say, 'We know what scripture means and don't need to raise anymore questions.' It is always a way of saying that the church in each generation must make fresh and rejuvenated efforts to understand scripture more fully and live by it more thoroughly, even if that means cutting across cherished traditions."[7]

Since, admit it or not, we interpret Scripture through our own lens of context and history and culture, we must learn more about culture and context for the Bible. We need to read it in the way that the writers meant it and the way their immediate recipients would have read it.

Perhaps, just perhaps, we can't read singular verses or chapters in a vacuum; perhaps we can't read letters written to specific people with specific situations in mind in a specific context and then apply them, broad-brush, to the whole of humanity or the church or even our own small selves. Perhaps we need wisdom, insight. We need the Holy Spirit. Perhaps we need

> We can't read letters written to specific people in a specific context and then apply them, broad-brush, to the whole of humanity or the church.

Jesus as our best and clearest lens; we need all of Scripture, too. After all, Jesus is the Word of God incarnate.

We'll likely also need some strong coffee.

If you are looking for the one key Bible verse that makes all of your wondering go away, I'm sorry to disappoint you. I had to chuckle while I was researching, because honestly, there is just so much material, and almost all of it contradicts itself and each other. And therein lies the problem and the root of the questions and issues that have gathered us here together. Even well-respected scholar Dr. Stackhouse writes candidly,

> I had been reading yet another explanation of 1 Timothy 2:11–15, easily one of the most obscure of the classic passages on this matter. I remember quite clearly now—more than twenty years later— putting the book down on my lap and realizing this insight: Nobody could explain this passage. To be sure, I had been reading more than a dozen attempts to explain this passage. Some of them were ingenious; a few were even likely. But it struck me with paradigm-shaking force that no one could explain all the clauses in this passage with full plausibility. I then began to think that this problem was true not only of expositions of this one text but of the whole gender question. No one I had read (and I had read quite a few) could put all the relevant

texts together into a single, finished puzzle with no pieces left over, with none manufactured to fill in gaps, and with none forced into place. . . . We should not wait to come to a theological conclusion until the happy day in which we have arranged all the relevant texts. Instead, we should look at all the texts as open-mindedly as possible and see if among the various competing interpretations there is one that makes the most sense of the most texts and especially the most important ones. . . . For what else can we do in theology?[8]

What else can we do now but this? We trust the Holy Spirit will lead us and guide us into all truth. We trust that we are his sheep, and we know the voice of our Shepherd. And then we do our best to work out what God has already worked in. So while I'm not going to expound in detail on every verse that mentions women in the New Testament—others do so much better than I could, and I've listed some of my source material in the back of this book—I do hope to provide you with a lens through which to see Scripture and hopefully set you off on a new journey through the Word on your own.

Let's dig in, shall we?

Women should be silent during the church meetings. It is not proper for them to speak. They should be submissive, just as the law says. If they have any ques-

*tions, they should ask their husbands at home, for it
is improper for women to speak in church meetings.*

1 Corinthians 14:34–35 (NLT)

*Women should learn quietly and submissively. I do
not let women teach men or have authority over
them. Let them listen quietly.*

1 Timothy 2:11–12 (NLT)

Now, take a deep breath. I know I just did.

Those Bible verses arrive with a steamer trunk of baggage
on your doorstep, don't they? As women, we often hear this
mandate to be submissive, to be silent, in the context of our
souls being crushed in big and small ways; and the arch of our
interpretations have real, hurtful, and sometimes dangerous
implications.

It's tempting to compactly tuck the roles of women into
these few lines of Scripture and shrug in resignation or tri-
umph: "Well, I didn't say it; God did."

I believe that all Scripture is God-breathed. And these passages? Hard words they seem, but yes—God-breathed. Yet our
scriptures are not a collection of 140-character tweets or cable
news headlines appropriate for digestion between celebrity
news and the weather.

The aforementioned verses are from the letters of Paul.

They are not an exhaustive list of rules and their exceptions. They are not universal standards without context and purpose.

No, they are a portion of the letters from the Apostle Paul, inspired by the Holy Spirit, written to specific people in specific cities for specific situations that had arisen. In these same types of letters, he asked for his cloak, reminded them of conversations, and sent along his personal greetings and affection. Just like our own letters between friends or family, there is a backstory and shared history to every letter, implied and understood.

The whole picture of the Church or Paul's ministry isn't to be found here in two verses. So these portions of Scripture, so often used to oppress women or refuse opportunity or give place to patriarchy, must be understood in the context of the whole of Scripture.

Women in the community of God were leading, teaching, ministering, and prophesying at the time of the letters Paul wrote to Timothy and to the Corinthian church. These women were doing this in fulfillment of the Apostle Peter's prophetic words in Acts 2:18: "In those days I will pour out my Spirit even on my servants—men and women alike—and they will prophesy." (NLT)

And women were doing these things with the full knowledge and apparent blessing of church leaders—including Paul. In fact, just a few verses earlier, in 1 Corinthians 14:39, Paul was *encouraging* the women of the church to prophesy alongside their brothers.

So perhaps his command for women to be silent isn't for all times, all places, all women?

It's helpful for me, in discerning the meaning of these passages, to turn to the rest of the writer's work. In a letter to the church in Galatia, Paul wrote, "There is no longer Jew or Gentile, slave or free, male and female. For you are all one in Christ Jesus."[9] This same idea was also shared with the church in Colossae when Paul wrote, "In this new life, it doesn't matter if you are a Jew or a Gentile, circumcised or uncircumcised, barbaric, uncivilized, slave, or free. Christ is all that matters, and he lives in all of us."[10]

John Stackhouse says it is crucial to understand that when Paul wrote these letters, he was giving the church a few instructions on how to "survive and thrive in a patriarchal culture that he thinks will not last long[11] and to maintain and promote the egalitarian dynamic already at work in the career of Jesus that in due course will leave gender lines behind."[12]

In Corinth, as everywhere the gospel was preached, women had flocked to the church, along with slaves, the poor, the weak, and children. It was revolutionary to be so valued, so loved, so cared for, so affirmed (which, for some of God's daughters, is not that hard to relate to right here and now).

When we look at these passages or letters through the lens of our egalitarian modern culture, sure—they seem like small potatoes, probably even offensive. But in a patriarchal culture, women were never included in the teaching, encouraged to prophesy, or given dignity as participants. Remember—this was a time when women were not well educated beyond the sphere of their duties at home, let alone in public worship and discussions. Many scholars believe that in the exhilaration of their newfound freedom, a group of women were disrupting the meeting with questions and opinions, and Paul, as a reminder, asked them to learn in quietness and talk it over at home with their husbands. The gatherings weren't quite the place for this.

Even Paul's recommendation that women should ask their husbands if they had questions was revolutionary for that time period. He was encouraging women to learn!—to ask questions, to seek out answers, to fully participate in the community. Everyone—including the Jews—excluded women from education, religious training, and participation (with the exception of temple prostitution in pagan worship).

But when Paul wrote this letter to the Corinthian church, they were in disunity and disorder. They were quarreling. He wrote to them, as a pastor and a friend, to deal with the spirit of division among them. In an effort to shut down the chaos attending the outbursts of prophesying, speaking in tongues, and women questioning or interrupting, some members of the church, rightfully longing for orderly worship, attempted to shut down these activities entirely. But as David Hamilton writes, Paul clearly "wanted everyone to be involved in the ministry of the church, each one contributing according to his or her ministry gifts," so he took the time to go through each of the disordered groups with specific corrections, and then he went back through them in reverse to "defend their right to communicate in an orderly fashion, correcting those who would silence them outright."[13]

Paul's intention was to restore order to the community of God. And that order didn't include the silencing of all women any more than it included a blanket forever-and-ever prohibition on prophesying or speaking in tongues.

> Paul's intention was to restore order to the community of God. And that order didn't include the silencing of all women.

Paul had the same expectations for women and men in the church. Youth With A Mission founder Loren Cunningham puts it this way: "You are free to minister, but you must do so responsibly. Stop ministering in a disorderly, disruptive, discourteous, insubordinate way. Your participation in the church must be done in an orderly way, submitting to God so that your ministry edifies the whole Body of Christ."[14]

Paul was passionate about teaching and training new believers—women included. He wanted each individual to use his or her gifts, strengthening the church. In that same passage of Scripture, he said he preferred to use those gifts in public that allowed him "to instruct others."[15] He urged them all—men and women—to grow toward spiritual maturity, to think as adults, not childishly. In Ephesians 4:21–24, Paul wrote "since you have heard about Jesus and have learned the truth that comes from him, throw off your old sinful nature and your former way of life, which is corrupted by lust and deception. Instead, let the Spirit renew your thoughts and attitudes. Put on your new nature, created to be like God—truly righteous and holy." (NLT)

In his letter to the Corinthians, quoted earlier in this chapter, Paul wrote for women to "submit," yes, but he did so without the lead-in of husbands. He also wrote "as the law says," but nowhere in Paul's Bible (the Old Testament) is there a law about women in the abstract submitting to men. Paul was a scholar and certainly would have known that no such law existed, and there is a possibility that he meant for women to submit to the Church, to God, or even to themselves, but not to men in the abstract.[16]

And the word *quietly* here in the letter to Timothy isn't actually *silence*, as mentioned in Corinthians. No, the Greek word is *hesuchia*, which means "stillness"—more along the lines of peacefulness or minding one's own business. It's not about talking versus not talking; it's about learning in a still way, far from meddling in other people's affairs. This word harmonizes with what we know of how women were behaving in this church at this time. Being able to learn in stillness, with peace, instead of in a clamor and with restlessness, or meddling, is a true gift to a student and learner. I never learn much myself when I'm constantly interrupting and questioning or applying the lesson to everyone else first. Sometimes, we learn most in our stillness and peace. But there is a big difference between "being silenced and silencing oneself," as Rachel Held Evans wisely points out.[17] So when Paul asked women to be silent, theologian and professor Scot McKnight writes in *The Blue Parakeet* that "he is not talking about ordinary Christian women; rather, he has a specific group of women in mind."[18] Paul was not silencing every woman in every circumstance for every age. Some scholars even translate the plural word "women" into the singular "woman," signaling that one specific woman was actually causing the trouble.[19]

Paul was not silencing every woman in every circumstance for every age.

When Paul referenced that Adam was created first, then Eve, in 1 Timothy 2:13, he wasn't assigning superiority to Adam based on birth order (if that were the case, animals win). No, he's pointing out Adam was there first, so he had something to teach Eve. She needed to learn. She wasn't inferior; she was ignorant, lacking in knowledge. Paul wanted the women of the church to remember that it's not an issue of inferiority but an issue of learning with a quiet spirit in humility as they had much to learn.[20]

Loren Cunningham writes,

So, should women be silent? Yes, just like the men. Should women be prepared to minister with "a hymn, or a word of instruction, a revelation, a tongue of interpretation"? Yes, just like the men.

Should women exercise self-control as they minister? Yes, just like the men. Should women seek to educate themselves so that they can better edify others when they minister? Yes, just like the men. "For God is not a God of disorder but of peace."[21]

When women are restricted from the service of God in any capacity, the Church is mistakenly allowing an imperfect male-dominated ancient culture to drive our understanding and practice of Christ's redeeming work, instead of Jesus Christ and the whole of the Scriptures.

In the context of the whole story of Scripture and the Church, let alone Paul's whole letters and activities, Paul didn't prohibit women from speaking or using their gifts within the community of God. This demonstrates what scholars have concluded: Paul's stated goal was that "everyone (regardless of gender) be instructed and encouraged. Paul was making sure that women were not left out of the process."[22]

It is crucial that we understand Paul's overall perspective on the role and place of women, as well as the specific context within which he wrote these particular portions of his letters. Paul commended women to prophesy, honored them in ministry, and counted them among his friends.

Paul believed women were people, too. As a follower of Jesus, of course he did. Of course he did.

"*I love that you get cold when it's 71 degrees out.*
I love that it takes you an hour and a half to order
a sandwich. I love that you get a little crinkle above your
nose when you're looking at me like I'm nuts.
I love that after I spend the day with you,
I can still smell your perfume on my clothes.
And I love that you are the last person I want to talk to
before I go to sleep at night."

When Harry Met Sally (screenplay written by Nora Ephron)

CHAPTER FIVE

Dancing Warriors

The first time Brian met my family was at my sister's high school graduation. He flew from Tulsa to Calgary in the chill days of our early summer, and we went to the convention center for the post–graduation ceremony dinner and family dance. Despite Brian's reluctance, I blithely pulled him out to the dance floor with me. He began to dance, and I began to laugh: "Oh, that's hilarious! You can stop kidding around! Let's really dance now."

He froze in the middle of the whirling couples and said, with as much dignity as he could muster, "That *was* me really dancing."

Oops.

We stood in that swirl of much-better-at-it-than-us danc-ers, laughing at each other until our sides ached. When the music switched to a slow song, he pulled me in, and we shuffled in a circle, clinging, still chuckling occasionally. A few months later, he asked me to marry him outside a fancy restaurant's se-cluded backyard forest, down on one knee in the darkness. We never had the courage or the money to go inside for a table.

We dutifully submitted to premarital counseling, and like any overachieving evangelical couple, we did extra reading of the popular marriage books about love and respect and boundaries, about sex and money and in-laws and commu-nication. We filled out reams of work sheets together. We sat through church retreats and sermons. Throughout our mar-riage, Brian has listened patiently to pleas from the pulpit about being "a real man" and "stepping up to be the spiritual leader" and "taking his place in his family." I suffered through the grief of our lost babies and wilted under Mother's Day sermons extolling the "true" or "real" women. (Wasn't I real enough?)

Brian makes me laugh, and he makes me think hard. He's a leader wherever he goes—always has been. His eyes follow only me when we are in a crowded room, and we can have en-tire conversations with one raised eyebrow. There isn't anyone else with whom we'd rather be alongside for the realities of raising a family, financial upheavals, desire, making a home, building a marriage, and walking in the narrow ways of Jesus.

We have gone to the high places and the lowest places of each other, crossing dry desert, drinking deep of the oasis, and we are still dancing.

My husband has forgiven me when I could not forgive myself for how I had hurt us. I have held him up when he was sinking in the mires, praying joy right back into him at night in our bed while he was sleeping. Sometimes—oh my—we can infuriate each other, and we're just *so different* from each other; but there is a bone-deep knowing that we—this marriage, all of it—are meant to be.

Our marriage is still more of that shuffling, laughing slow dance than a carefully choreographed ballroom performance. We move slowly, my head on his heart, his breath in my hair, his hands on my wider-than-they-used-to-be hips; our feet are slower, perhaps because we're moving together. We are always moving through life together, helping each other become more like the Jesus we love.

Over the years, we have discovered that this is another way to move within marriage, and yes—it's very different than the traditional and stifling language of roles, headship, submission, and soft patriarchy found within many Christian marriage books and seminars.

We began to realize that the development and growth in our marriage and the way we lived our lives were not an evidence of what some might call a "Jezebel spirit" in me or his "lack of spiritual leadership"; no, the oneness and mutuality in our marriage was actually evidence of the Holy Spirit at work.[1]

Mutuality is a beautiful picture of trust and a sign of the King-dom of God.

Sometimes the questions people ask or judgments they imply make us chuckle.

Well, who is in charge here?

We are.

Yes, but if push comes to shove, who is the leader?

We are.

But then who is the spiritual head of your home?

Only Jesus. Only ever our Jesus.

Like many other Christians throughout the ages, we believe Scripture teaches mu-tual submission in marriage, and so we strive for our mar-riage to be a reflection of the original God-created order— we endeavor to make our mar-riage a restoration of oneness, of equality, of two lives in the concert of playing second fiddle to one another; we are allies and restored image bearers slow dancing here beside the rocks in the light of the moon, affirming the truth that every mar-riage is as unique as the image bearers within the covenant.

> **Like many other Christians through the ages, we believe Scripture teaches mutual submission in marriage.**

IN THE NEW Testament, the most-quoted instructions for mar-riage are given within the context of cultural household "codes" or structures.

Wives, submit yourselves to your own husbands as you do to the Lord. For the husband is the head of the wife as Christ is the head of the church, his body, of which he is the Savior. Now as the church submits to Christ, so also wives should submit to their husbands in everything.

Ephesians 5:22–24 (NIV)

Wives, submit yourselves to your husbands, as is fitting in the Lord. Husbands, love your wives and do not be harsh with them.

Colossians 3:18–19 (NIV)

Wives, in the same way submit yourselves to your own husbands so that, if any of them do not believe the word, they may be won over without words by the behavior of their wives, when they see the purity and reverence of your lives.

1 Peter 3:1–2 (NIV)

The Greco-Roman household codes, in effect at the time of the New Testament, were another link in a heavy chain of patriarchy extending throughout history. Since patriarchy and hierarchy were consequences of the Fall, these systems were built into the code because the maintaining of total authority in the home was critical to the functioning of a society that relied on the total authority of the government and/or religion. And at the time of the New Testament writings on marriage, the Greco-Roman household codes were part of Pax Romana law. So these select verses of teachings for wives (and children and slaves) line up with the law of the land.

And yet in context, these passages also continue the pattern of subversion without revolution. Peter and Paul worked within imperfect systems because "with Roman officials looking for every excuse to imprison Christians, any challenge would bring scrutiny and persecution for the early Church." The Apostles "advocated this system, not because God had revealed it as the divine will for Christian homes, but because it was the only stable and respectable system anyone knew about" at the time, according to Carol A. Newsom and Sharon H. Ringe of the *Women's Bible Commentary*.[2]

Paul and Peter used the codes as metaphors or scaffolding because they were familiar and daily, not because they were prescriptive or ideal. These passages were actually subversive in their time because they placed demands on the assumed power of men (teaching them to be kind to their slaves, to be gentle with their children, to love their wives) and because they addressed the most powerless in a patriarchal society—the women, the children, the slaves. The Church attracted the powerless in droves—Celsus famously declared in the second century that "Christianity is a religion for women, children, and slaves"—and so this spin on the codes was unheard of in the culture.[3] Peter's and Paul's words line up with the bigger truths of the whole story of Scripture, particularly the life of Jesus, guiding our interpretations.

Life in Christ is not meant to mirror life in a Greco-Roman culture. An ancient Middle Eastern culture is not our standard. We are not meant to adopt the world of Luther's Reformation or the culture of the eighteenth-century Great Awakening or even 1950s America as our standard for righteousness. The culture, past or present, isn't the point: Jesus and his Kingdom come, his will done, right now—that is the point.

Since we're talking about context, it may help if we talk a bit about Creation too. God called the first woman *ezer*—a name he embraces for himself throughout the Old Testament. Yes, in the garden, God created woman out of Adam's side, and he named his daughter after himself. The word that accompanies *ezer* is *kenegdo*, typically translated as "suitable" or "helpmeet." I'm sure we've all heard a teaching or two on the word *helpmeet*, focused on woman as a man's assistant as wife, mother, and homemaker. But as Carolyn Custis James insightfully points out, this traditional and narrow view "excludes 60 percent of females in this country [the United States] alone. How many millions of women and girls are we leaving out worldwide? Focus on the wife as her husband's helper has led to the belief that God gave primary roles and responsibilities to men, and secondary, supporting roles to women. It has led to practices that communicate that women are second-class citizens at home and in the church."[4]

Ezer kenegdo actually means man's perfect match, explains Rachel Held Evans.[5] It is the help that opposes, two parts of equal weight leaning against one another. Biblical scholar and theologian, Victor P. Hamilton writes, "[Kenegdo] suggests that what God creates for Adam will correspond to him. Thus the new creation will be neither a superior nor an inferior but an equal. The creation of this helper will form one-half of a polarity, and will be to man as the South Pole is to the North Pole. She will be his strongest ally in pursuing God's purposes and his first roadblock when he veers off course."[6]

In the Old Testament, the word *ezer* appears twenty-one times in three different contexts: the creation of woman, when Israel applied for military aid, and in reference to God as Israel's helper for military purposes (in this context, *ezer* appears sixteen times).[7] God isn't a helpmeet in the watered-down milquetoast way we've taught or understood that word within our churches, is he? No, our God is more than that: he's a *strong* helper, a warrior.

By naming his daughters after this aspect of his character, God did not name women as secondary helpmeet *assistants*. No, friend—women were created and called out as *warriors*.

You, sister—did you know? You are a warrior, alongside your

> You are a warrior, alongside your brothers, on God's mission in the world.

brothers, on God's mission in the world. Brother, did you know? You have an ally; you aren't in this alone. And this calling of fellow warriors is not exclusive to husbands and wives in a marriage relationship: men and women together in the Kingdom of God are allies.

Neither one of us—woman or man—is secondary or backup; we are all key parts of Kingdom building, intrinsic to the story of God, right now.

Throughout Scripture, we see women of valor, women operating in their anointing and created purpose as *ezer kenegdo*. We'll talk about this more a bit later on, but I want you to know this right now: we have a lineage and legacy of Church mothers, women of God, who were warriors in the situations where God placed them, in ways unique to their temperament and character, callings, gifting, and even choices. Women of God live with valor. Paul called the Church—men and women—to put on the full armor of God.

In the early new light of Creation, God didn't set up a "masculine" rule as his standard and plan for humanity. No, it was masculine and feminine, together, bearing the image of God. New Testament scholar at Fuller Seminary J. R. Daniel Kirk says, "Only this kind of shared participation in representing God's reign to the world is capable of doing justice to the God whose image we bear."[8]

As we live in a world desperate for a glimpse of God, desperate for rescue, crushed by evil and poverty and war and the grind of lonely existence in quiet desperation, we, the Church, are part of God's plan to push back that darkness and make room for his Kingdom. We are commissioned to multiply his image bearers, care for the poor, and minister life and hope and healing in the name of Jesus, to the glory of God.

If a woman is held back, minimized, pushed down, or downplayed, she is not walking in the fullness God intended for her as his image bearer, as his *ezer* warrior. If we minimize our gifts, hush our voice, and stay small in a misguided attempt to fit a weak and culturally conditioned standard of femininity, we cannot give our brothers the partner they require in God's mission for the world.

The kind of help a man needs demands full deployment of all we are as women—no holding back. Men are most truly "helped" when women give our best. As Carolyn Custis James points out, "His life will change for the better because of what she contributes to his life. Together they will daily prove in countless and surprising ways that two is always better than one."[9]

And men, what a gift for you! What a revelation! A man does not need to deny a woman's identity as a beloved and unique warrior in Christ out of misplaced fear or insecurity or a hunger for power. Let's praise God together for his truth. Sons, brothers, husbands, friends, can you imagine? God knew that it was not good for you to be alone, and he gave you your best ally. You were never intended to do the work of God—in your home, in your church, in a lost and dying world—alone. You were given allies, partners, warriors, and lovers in the form of women. Throughout Scripture and world history, we see the richness of partnership between men and women as God intended when he created them together: man and woman he created them.

Jesus ushered in a crazy upside-down Kingdom of voluntary submission and love, a Kingdom where the least is the most honored and the one who gives everything is the one who gains it all. This is the Kingdom of love, a Kingdom without a score-sheet tally or grabs for power. This is a Kingdom without envy and bitterness, and in our relationships with one another, we strive to have "the same mindset as Christ Jesus: Who, being in very nature God, did not consider equality with God something to be used to his own advantage; rather, he made himself nothing by taking the very nature of a servant, being made in human likeness. And being found in appearance as a man, he humbled himself by becoming obedient to death—even death on a cross!"[10]

We're still like the Sons of Thunder, aren't we? "Lord, but who's in charge? Who will be the greatest?"[11] And whether we're talking about our own selves or our callings or our roles in our marriages or churches, I imagine the response is, "Anyone who becomes as humble as this little child is the greatest in the Kingdom of Heaven." Or perhaps, "Anyone who wants to be first must be last, and the greatest is the servant of all."[12]

And if our marriages can give some small and imperfect glimpse of the Kingdom of God in action, warriors fighting in distinct unity, then we need to dance, in and around and with each other, in intimacy and mutual submission. Theologians throughout church history have used the term *perichoresis*, a Greek word meaning "an indwelling," to describe the relationship of and between the Trinity. Perichoresis is far past fellowship; it's the center of intimacy, a cleaving together born of friendship and love. Mystical and divine, it's an imperfect metaphor, yet there is no hierarchy, only more love; there is a breathing after one another and a making room for the other. The Trinity "works" by never-ending giving to each other and the receiving of the other out of each other. It's a procession of togetherness in the blur of oneness.[13]

When Paul likened marriage to the relationship between Christ and the Church in Ephesians 5:23–28, it was not an exhortation to hierarchy and power structures. Christ's relationship with us as the Church is characterized by his crazy love and sacrificial giving, not power grabbing. Paul's words remind us that Christ gave himself up for the Church, cleansed her, and loved her.

> **When Paul likened marriage to the relationship between Christ and the Church, it was not an exhortation to hierarchy and power structures.**

And so we discover the great paradox hidden within these hotly debated passages of Scripture, tragically misused to subject and berate and hold back, to demand and give place to pride—however benevolent the intention. If wives submit to their husbands as the Church submits to Christ, and if husbands love their wives as Christ loved the Church and gave himself up for her, and if both husbands and wives submit to one another as commanded, we enter a never-ending, life-giving circle of mutual submission and love.

We are able to offer our "You first, darling" as an overflow of the completeness we enjoy in Jesus. The submission of Christ is gospel centered, aligned with God's purposes, a pouring out of himself to rescue a lost humanity.[14] Submission in a healthy marriage between two people walking together in the Way follows that same trajectory: it requires tenacity, strength, and courage of the bravest sort. But there is a vast difference between mutual submission to one another out of an overflow of love and respect and having submission demanded of you as a husband's right, isn't there?

Marriage within the Kingdom of God isn't an exercise in authority and headship—let alone a laundry list of roles and rules and responsibilities and chore divisions or the profanity of abuse and subjection. Marriage is a beautiful example of oneness and cooperation, an image of the dance of the Trinity in perfect unity.

So even though we are terrible dancers, Brian and I decided in the early days to learn to hold on and dance our way through our marriage.

He leads, and I lead. We are both following the music of the Ancient One; there is no hierarchy between us. We move together, one body, all for intimacy and beauty. We are in the vast middle of our love story still; we know every curve of each other, but we are leaning into the unknown parts with full trust.

I trust my husband completely—with every bit of our life and with myself. My trust is not because I must, not because I believe God commands me to submit without question to his leadership because I am easily deceived or weak. I submit because I am walking in the Way of Jesus. As a man of God, Brian serves me, too.

So Brian follows me when I step out into a new place. And I know just when to slide into my turn as the shadow; but we've stomped on each other's toes a time or two, been horribly out of step—oh yes. Sometimes he leads; sometimes I lead. It changes because our relationship is alive and organic, still developing—but it's always us, trusting each other's heart, trusting we hear the same music from that old piano. We're still learning to move seamlessly together. If we can't move together, then we wait, holding on, in the pause between steps.

Marriage is an intimate embrace masquerading as a dance. We love a chance to be close, especially in these middle chapters of our love story, when we feel more like a blur of tasks and responsibilities in romance. (It seems every time we hug now, we're tackled by a trio of tinies bellowing, "Family hug!")

If marriage truly is a glimpse of grace drawing near, then may it be a glimpse of mutuality, giving, love, and intimacy. And if all we ever accomplish with our marriages is the loving of each other down through the years, that's enough, and it's a real marriage.[15]

Live in me. Make your home in me, just as I do in you.
In the same way that a branch can't bear grapes by itself
but only by being joined to the vine,
you can't bear fruit unless you are joined with me.
I am the vine, you are the branches.
When you're joined with me and I with you,
the relation intimate and organic,
the harvest is sure to be abundant.

John 15:4–5 (MSG)

CHAPTER SIX

Patron Saints, Spiritual Midwives, and "Biblical" Womanhood

Throughout the years, we have walked through seasons in our marriage. I have been a full-time working mother and a part-time working mother. There were seasons when we both worked full-time in separate careers; then there was that one year when my husband was the primary caregiver and homemaker for us as he finished seminary, and I put him through school. For right now, anyway, I am a stay-at-home mum, and I write a little on the edges of my life, while Brian works full-time.

87

At no time in all of those seasons of our marriage have we felt more "biblical" than in any other season.

Did we feel happier or saner or more settled in certain seasons with certain decisions based on what works best for our family? Yes, absolutely.

But were we more Christian or more biblical, based on our employment status or chores? No.

I'm not quite sure when the Church decided that "biblical" was the perfect adjective for subjective roles and situations. I don't think it's helped us. Usually when people use that phrase, they are thinking more about June Cleaver than the early church's Lydia, described as being "diligent in business," or perhaps a sanitized sitcom society that never actually existed instead of Deborah, the military strategist of Israel, let alone Junia, a respected apostle alongside Paul.

When I discovered I was pregnant with our eldest daughter, Anne, I went shopping the very next day—not to a baby superstore, floor to ceiling with all the items you never knew you needed to raise a scrap of humanity. Nope—I ran to the bookstore, one of my first temples.

I wandered the aisles, dreaming of the day when I would again read these beloved children's books, picking out my favorites: *Stuart Little*, *Charlotte's Web*, the Ramona books, the Little House on the Prairie series, *Caddie Woodlawn*, the Chronicles of Narnia, *The Wonderful Wizard of Oz*, and don't even get me started on the Anne of Green Gables books (after all, we named our eldest daughter Anne with an *e*). Now three tinies and one crowded couch later, we read aloud as a family every night.

One night, when she was six years old, Anne brought home a book from her public school library. *Every-Day Dress-Up* is a picture book written by a mother admittedly sick of reading Disney princess stories and longing to expose her daughter to female role models who were brave and strong pioneers. I was thrilled at Anne's choice, and we passed a happy evening reading the book. She was enthralled by the stories of real women. We looked up information on the Internet about each one of them. She wanted to see them "in real life" and was plainly pleased that Amelia Earhart had a similar haircut to her own. We danced to Ella Fitzgerald's "At Last" and marveled at Frida Kahlo's paintings.[1]

As part of our family reading habits, we include Bible stories. Remember how I grew up with Scripture woven into the fabric of our family? Because the practice has enriched my life in every way, I am attempting to give our tinies the same legacy. We read from the *Jesus Storybook Bible* by Sally Lloyd-Jones, along with a few picture books based on heroes of the faith and oft-told Bible stories. I began to search for faith-based picture books, in particular a few with female lead characters. Most of what I found wasn't that different from the stories for girls in the mass market: pink, sparkles, cupcakes, princesses, dress-up. "Boy" books featured knights and princes, battles and heroics. There isn't anything wrong with those things— heaven knows we enjoy some of those stories and activities here—but I did long for more than stereotypes about the experiences and adventures of men and women following in the ways of Jesus.

It's not a conspiracy theory. The status quo is simply what sells—mass market or Christian market—and so we stick with the familiar, and we buy another kids' book about David and Goliath, another book about the princess with a chaste message about not kissing or a rescue with a Jesusy spin on it. Meanwhile, women influence our faith, have adventures, and make hard choices—we all know it because we all experience it; yet they don't get the shelf space they deserve. I wanted those stories.

If I owned a bookstore, it would look like The Shop Around the Corner in the Meg Ryan and Tom Hanks movie, *You've Got Mail*. (I should confess that most of my home decorating decisions come down to one question: *Would this belong in Kathleen Kelly's little New York brownstone?* If it's a yes, then *in it goes*.) I would build an extra shelf just for the stories of women, to read and pass out right alongside their brothers in the faith, the Church fathers and Church mamas, and I'd say, "Look at what we can do together. Here, sit in the beanbag chair for a while and read about Corrie ten Boom."

I'd probably label that shelf "Patron Saints" or "Spiritual Midwives" to explain how I feel about the people intrinsically linked to my spiritual journey. It's an imperfect metaphor, but in a way, it's like they helped give birth to some new part of me. Maybe they were the midwives—by their lives, their faith, their obedience, their work, their prayers—for the work that God has birthed in me and through me, and countless others.

And I rise up and call blessed the women who have *mothered*—nurtured, nourished, sourced, watched over—my spiritual journey. Most of them won't ever know that they influenced me as much as they did, but it's true. God used them powerfully in my life, and they did that simply by living their own lives in obedience to God, regardless of crowds or sales figures or proper titles.

We could take some time tonight for the women, you and me. Our Bible pages, our church history, our own lives are filled with puzzle pieces of the midwifery of the Kingdom.

> Our Bible pages, our church history, our own lives are filled with puzzle pieces of the midwifery of the Kingdom.

There's Eve, mother of us all, the first true partner, walking in the full equality God intended, the corresponding character, the other part of God's image on earth alongside Adam. And yet Eve is often cast as the villain in the simplifying of our fall-from-grace story, instead of the enemy of all our souls, the devil. The curse that was laid upon Eve—her desire would be for her husband, and her pain in childbirth would be greatly multiplied—even shows us how patriarchy, subordination, and pain are part of the Fall. They were never God's original intent; they are a consequence of sin.[2]

Deborah was a judge and a prophet of Israel during a

bloody and intense period of conflict for the nation of Israel.[3] Rachel Held Evans says she walked in complete "religious, political, judicial, and militaristic authority over the people of Israel. She was essentially Israel's commander in chief."[4] When Barak, a warrior, doubted her instructions, she called his bluff by going along with him and receiving the honor for the victory. Plus, she told him that because he doubted, their enemy's great general Sisera would be delivered into the hands of a woman. Sure enough, after Israel won the battle, Sisera ran to hide in a tent. Waiting in the tent was Jael. She waited until Sisera fell asleep and then murdered him with a tent peg to the skull. Two women as two ancient warriors. Often when a woman exhibits leadership, she's accused of having that Jezebel spirit. I look forward to the day when women with leadership and insight, gifts and talents, callings and prophetic leanings are called out and celebrated as a Deborah, instead of silenced as a Jezebel.

I'd add some books about the Old Testament women like Ruth, who broke the rules but honored God; Rahab of Jericho, who hid the Israelite spies and saved her family during the siege; and, of course, Esther, who saved the Jews. I would tuck in a few pages for Abigail, who captured David's heart; Hannah, who gave her son Samuel to God; and Tamar, who outsmarted dishonorable men to defend herself. I would include the stories of the victims of patriarchy, the nameless daughters of Jerusalem will be remembered.

In the first-century Christian Church, Priscilla was one

part of a powerhouse couple, beside her husband, Aquila.[5] The Apostle Paul partnered with them as tent makers by trade, and he had full confidence in them. They risked their necks on his behalf once, and he was always grateful. When they heard the eloquent evangelist Apollos teaching in the synagogue of Ephesus, they brought him home to correct some of his teaching and then sent him back out again. Priscilla and Aquila are always mentioned as a pair, oftentimes with Priscilla's name first, indicating their mutuality in the relationship and leadership. In fact, Priscilla may have been the author of the book of Hebrews, according to some scholars.[6] Eventually both Priscilla and Aquila gave their lives as martyrs for the sake of the gospel. There is a long history of women ministering alongside their husbands, in the fullness of their unique gifts, as a team.

Then there's elderly Anna the Prophetess, who was only mentioned once in Scripture.[7] She was an longtime widow, having lost her husband after only seven years of marriage. She spent the rest of her life at the temple, worshipping and fasting day and night. On the day that Mary and Joseph brought Jesus to the temple for his dedication, she was there. She recognized him and called out the truth. This is the mark of a soul in pursuit of Jesus: we recognize him. He's there in the stuff of the soul, the tendrils of the spirit. We're like those who dream of home, but, like Anna, we know—the truth is there in our hearts the whole time. We see glimpses of him, and we have a holy hunch. He drifts like smoke or storms in like flashes of lightning insight or takes our breath when he appears even as a tiny baby in our own temples. We have these moments of transcendence, as if the thin veil between heaven and earth is fluttering in the most normal and ordinary moments of our lives, and then we can't breathe for the loveliness of the world and each other, and just like that, *our souls remember something; we recognize him here.*

So Anna recognized him because of her years of longing for him, and she spent the rest of her life telling them all that she held him in her arms, her own arms. I love Anna because of her faithfulness despite the fact that life didn't turn out as she likely had planned. She was widowed early in life, and then she went to the temple as a prophetess and ministers, and she was faithful to her calling anyway. And then—with her own aged eyes—she saw him.

Lydia was a respected and wealthy businesswoman, apparently independent, and a leader in the early Church.[8] She financially supported the work of the apostles, was the first European convert, and welcomed Paul and his companions into her own home. Her home became a central gathering place for the church in Philippi. The Orthodox Church even considers her "equal with the apostles" for her work, and I consider her a spiritual mama because she consciously worked at her chosen vocation to, and for, the glory of God. I often think of Lydia when people argue over the false dichotomy of whether or not women should work. Women have always worked; they will always work—for their families, for their homes, for survival, for provision, for the good of their souls. It's a straw man argument for the purposes of arguing or imposing a new law. Lydia used her portion, a considerable business acumen and subsequent wealth, for the benefit of the gospel.

There are the women of Jesus' time on earth, whom we met in chapter 1: Mary, Martha, the woman with the issue of blood, the Samaritan woman, and Mary Magdalene. I've always had a soft spot for Martha, myself. And then there are the ministry partners of Chloe's[9] household, and Tryphena, Persis, and Tryphosa,[10] and Euodia and Syntyche who labored together with Paul.[11] Philip's four daughters were all prophets.[12]

Junia was an apostle of the early Church.[13] Paul wrote, "Greet Andronicus and Junia, my fellow Jews who have been in prison with me. They are outstanding among the apostles, and they were in Christ before I was." To be outstanding among the apostles, particularly as a woman, was high praise indeed.

There are the women of Church history like Florence Nightingale, who pioneered the modern nursing profession; Mother Teresa, who battled her own doubts and fears to serve relentlessly among the poor of India; Dorothy Day, the tireless social activist; Harriet Tubman, abolitionist and former slave who rescued hundreds of enslaved African Americans through the Underground Railroad; and Amy Carmichael, an Irish missionary to India who eventually founded a residential home for homeless children, particularly young girls rescued from temple prostitution. Corrie ten Boom, who defied the Nazis and defied bitterness ever afterward; the Salvation

Army's Evangeline Booth; and missionary to China Gladys Aylward, whose work covered everything from orphan care to prison reform—and on and on and on we go.

Gather our sisters to your memory's imaginary bookshelf.

Then there are the writers and thinkers who somehow mother me: Luci Shaw, Madeleine L'Engle, Kathleen Norris, Anne Lamott, Lauren Winner, Jen Hatmaker, Rachel Held Evans, Phyllis Tickle, and L. M. Montgomery—all so different from each other and all faithful in their way.

Then I have my mother, of course. My younger sister, Amanda, has walked all of my life beside me; she's my truest kindred-spirit soul friend. I have my Auntie Donna and my gone-too-soon grannies, Lorna and Nellie, and my mother-in-law, Leona. I have had women in my faith communities like Janet, Ruthanne, Karen, Julie, Eloise, Tracy, Natalie, Lisa, and so many more. I have plenty of "little sisters" in the faith, too—young women whom I "mentored" throughout the years (these girls all wound up teaching me more than I taught them). I have my heart-sister-writer tribe, a few soul-sisters, my church community, and a few good friends. I have my own tinies, who teach me more about God's ways and heart for humanity than any book I've read, and they have all made mothering the greatest crucible of my life, my primary altar for meeting with God.

Then there are the thousands of unnamed, unnoticed women in our global lineage of faith, the ones famous in heaven, and there are also the ones lost or trampled in history's march, to the cross fire of our world's sins and circumstance. I honor them, too.

What could I call this but a congregation of saints?

Don't you see? I had the stories already. And you have your stories, your own spiritual mamas and midwives, your own patron saints.

We don't need a sanctioned bookstore shelf or a marketing plan from a publishing house for the stories that shape us in ways big and small. We can tell their stories out loud.

Right alongside the stories of David and Moses and Paul, of Luther and Calvin, of Bonhoeffer and our dads, we could tell the stories of our own patron saints, our church mamas, our Kingdom midwives, the women of the Bible, and the women of the Word walking among us right now.

We simply need to tell our stories to our daughters and sons and to our friends, to each other here, and to our communities. The world could hear us rising up and calling them blessed in the city gates; we need to make room for the telling of their stories.

And so of course we won't define "biblical womanhood" well using a list of chores or a job description, a schedule or an income level. After all, healthy God-glorifying homes look as different as the image bearers that entered into the covenant, and biblical doesn't mean a baptized version of any culture, ancient or modern.

No, I am a biblical woman because I live and move and have my being in the daily reality of being a follower of Jesus, living in the reality of being loved, in full trust of my Abba. I am a biblical woman because I follow in the footsteps of all the biblical women who came before me.

Biblical womanhood isn't so different from biblical personhood. Biblical personhood becomes a dead list of rules when it becomes a law to keep. If we have a long list of rules—*Put others first! Be generous! Give money! Believe this! Do that!*—it's a dead religion from a glorified rule book.

> **Biblical womanhood isn't so different from biblical personhood.**

When our hearts, minds, and souls are deep within the reality of living loved, we discover that most of those "rules" from Sunday school are simply our new characteristics and our family traits. They are the fruit born of a meaningful, life-changing relationship—they are the flowers of life in the Vine. And there are many expressions and ways to live out love, joy, peace, kindness, patience, gentleness, faithfulness, self-control, and goodness—as men, as women, as wives, as husbands, as mothers, as fathers, as friends, as disciples. Marriage and motherhood are not the only way to biblical womanhood, as we see in so many of our spiritual mamas, despite our collective evangelical habit of treating single women and men as our personal match-making mission field.

Yes, I find God in the quotidian rhythms of my life as a wife and mother. I gain tremendous satisfaction from managing my household and raising my tinies to love God and love people.

But the doing of those things isn't making me a biblical woman. In the Church today, Carolyn Custis James warns that we can define womanhood:

> solely in terms of marriage and motherhood [and that simply does not fit] the reality of most of our lives. Even for those women who enthusiastically embrace marriage and motherhood as their highest calling, a substantial part of their lives is without a husband and/or children. A message that points to the marriage altar as the starting gate of God's calling for women leaves us with nothing to tell them except that God's purpose for them is not here and now, but somewhere down the road.[14]

Our acceptability as women before God is not dependent on our fathers or our husbands or the lack thereof.

In Christ, there is no such a narrow descriptor of biblical women—dependent on roles and chores, job descriptions and marital status, quieting our wisdom and intellect and voices, experiences and unique circumstances—when the majority of women in our world do not have the luxury of deciding whether or not to work. Women often must work to survive, to provide for their children. Throughout the centuries, women have worked in the fields and in their gardens and communities—from the agrarian age through the industrial and technological ages. The phenomenon of being a stay-at-home mother is relatively new and unique to the prosperous, right along with day cares to provide child care. It's a mark of our privilege to be able to decide (or make adjustments to our household budget) to keep one parent at home full-time with the children. I believe that is a worthy pursuit, good work, holy work (I hope so—it's my own daily work!), but it's not the same thing as biblical womanhood, is it? If the title can't be enjoyed by a woman in Haiti, or even by the women hailed in Scripture, the same way it can by a middle-class woman in Canada, then biblical womanhood must be more than this.

We are not biblical women because we achieve status as a stay-at-home mother and home-cook every meal. We are not men of God because we alone make the "hard decisions" and exclusively provide for our families, let alone because together we live out some version of a Greco-Roman household code. We are not living biblically by stuffing our true gifts and callings and passions into worn-out clichés, turning scriptural encouragement and invitations into new rules.

Our work in this life grows from the tree of his great love for us, birthed out of a growing and real relationship with Love itself. The organic blossoming of the fruit of the Spirit is only because of our life in the Vine. Whether we turn to the right or to the left, our ears will hear a voice behind, saying, "This is the way; walk in it."[15]

As we follow in the footsteps of our Savior, we are led away from the world's way of looking at life and conflict, community and creation, marriage and children, aging and youth, suffering and friendship. As we are faithful to each step, each nudge of the Holy Spirit's counsel, of life in Christ, of the counsel of Scripture, we find out that we end up right where we were meant to be all along, usually in the craziest of places. And we understand that it has been only through the work of the Spirit; no person could accomplish the wild and inclusive purposes of God.

In my black-and-white-rhetoric-only years, I struggled with understanding or accepting the tensions of God. I struggled with the Both-And nature of most of God's work and character, preferring the linear Either-Or.

He is both just and loving, the Lion and the Lamb. He is truth and grace. We practice works and live by faith. We are in God's Kingdom and not yet living in the fullness of heaven today. By his stripes we are healed, and our suffering perfects our faith. Men and women are equal in worth and value, and yet we are servants of one another. Jesus tells us God is our tender and good Father, and yet in other metaphors, he is more akin to a Lover. Our marriages are a symbol of Christ and the Church, and yet according to Paul, it's better to remain single. The paradoxes of the Christian faith abound, and they used to drive me a bit crazy.

The paradoxes of the Christian faith abound, and they used to drive me a bit crazy.

Because, well, which one *is* it? We want to know because then we would have a new law and new mandate, and life would be so much easier. Life is tidier with myths and rules;

the complex realities of the countercultural life in the Vine living are what baffle.

Edicts are easier than nudges. Scrolling ticker tapes are clearer than old scrolls, and in our religion-addled concepts of God as our get-out-of-hell card or an angry Judge, we can't conceive of an invitation to real relationship within the peace—the shalom—of a good God.

God doesn't call us to a new law. Abba invites us to the banquet tables, to communion, to community, and to life in the Vine—not to a religious treadmill or a life of conformity to someone else's best-case scenario. He calls us to intimate relationship with himself.

He calls us to a living, breathing working out of what he has already worked in. It is not accomplished by the work of our own selves, dutifully applying principles in seven subtitled paragraphs from a quick skim read. God's purposes in our individual lives, in our families, in our communities, in our cities, in our world are accomplished by the mysterious work of the Spirit in our hearts and minds, by the living and active Word of God, choice by choice, in freedom and community.

It takes practice. It starts with the smallest of moments of life. And it starts with this question: What would Love want to do here?

Love never gives up.
Love cares more for others than for self.
Love doesn't want what it doesn't have.

Love doesn't strut,
Doesn't have a swelled head,
Doesn't force itself on others,
Isn't always "me first,"
Doesn't fly off the handle,
Doesn't keep score of the sins of others,
Doesn't revel when others grovel,
Takes pleasure in the flowering of truth,
Puts up with anything,
Trusts God always,
Always looks for the best,
Never looks back,
But keeps going to the end.[16]

But again, this is not a list of rules; we are not reading an impossible standard—no. This describes our Jesus. This! This is our Abba. This is our Holy Spirit. He never gives up, and he takes pleasure in the flowering of truth.

And when we are following in the ways of Jesus, when we are abiding in the Vine, these become our characteristics, and we become signposts, tastes, movements of the Kingdom to the North, a glimpse of true Love. We embody the incarnation, the whole truth of Scripture, in our neighborhoods, among our neighbors, and even, most wild perhaps, in our own selves.

I have found the paradox,
that if you love until it hurts,
there can be no more hurt, only more love.

Mother Teresa

CHAPTER SEVEN

A Narrative Reborn

E ven though I have spent much of my life studying traditions, theology, and translations of Scripture, as well as bouncing in and out of all the iterations and denominations and factions of our crazy and divided spiritual lineage, I still don't know how to live my life except on my haunches at the feet of Jesus, eyes fixed on his face. Nothing else "works." No formula, no method makes me feel so fully human and alive as the radical act of living loved.[1] Once you taste Love, you are ruined for the empty shells of religious performance and conditions, like going back to fast food after a home-cooked meal eaten after a good day's work. Who went back to the dregs of the first bottles at the wedding in Cana instead of raising their glasses with the new wine, the best saved for last?

I had glimpses of what it meant to live my life this way, this connected vine sort of way, throughout my childhood and my growing-up years, even in early adulthood. Or I thought I knew what it meant. But for me, the truth of this way of life was learned, down to my bones, through my experiences of mothering.

It was a long road to the arrival of our three tinies: miscarriages, loss, sin, forgiveness—yearning unfulfilled, hope deferred. Five years into our marriage, we were at a place where our church leadership was wounded, our friends were hurting, lives were breaking apart. Right at a time of crisis in our church, we were supposed to lead a team of twenty-four teenagers to Europe on a mission trip. Nothing in our lives felt stable, our hearts were sorely bruised, and we were burned out.

And then we found ourselves expecting a baby.

It took a few days for it to sink in, and then we were so happy and hopeful. We were suddenly dreaming of our baby, vetoing each other's favorite names with laughter, imagining our spare bedroom as a nursery, making and adjusting our plans for this small unexpected and yet so welcome life.

I told Brian this baby was a gift from God, a special kiss from heaven just for us, for such a time as this. I waxed philosophic about new life, new beginnings, and all that.

We did not tell a soul except our parents. The plan was to keep it quiet for another week, until we were twelve weeks along and home from the trip. Two days before we were to leave for Europe, I went for my first ultrasound, a routine date confirmation. The technician looked at the screen. Then she said matter-of-factly, like we were discussing the weather, "Well, it doesn't look like this baby will live. It will probably be dead in a week or two. Let's book you for a D&C."[2]

That night, we lay on the floor in our bedroom; we couldn't even manage to get into the bed or onto the couch. Brian was flat on his back crying, tears pooling in his ears, while the ceiling fan hummed above us. I was curled up against him, soaking his shirt with my sorrow. We wanted to call our fellow pastors, we wanted to call our friends, and we wanted to cancel the trip. I unpacked and then repacked our suitcases over and over. We felt horribly, terribly alone in our grief; it was yet another loss in this season of never-ending loss, and I felt I could not bear it.

But in my fear, in my pride, and in my distrust of community, we told no one. I called the doctor's office and canceled the D&C, gently explaining that I could not be the one to say when the pregnancy was over. If it was going to end, it was going to be naturally—that decision felt right for me. The doctor's office staff made it clear to me: I was foolish.

The next morning, we were at the church, organizing the team, reassuring parents, checking passports, calming overly dramatic teenagers, loading luggage, and then flying from San Antonio to Minneapolis to Heathrow to Bonn. We were far from home, in the throes of yet another womb-deep sorrow.

I loved those teenagers like family. I still don't know if they could possibly understand how much comfort we drew from their normalcy, their weirdness, even their rebelliousness, during the days ahead. Every distraction, every mission-trip disaster was cause for relief. I wandered through the markets on cobblestone streets, I ate cherries outside of Beethoven's childhood home, I withdrew, performing the minimum of supervision and leadership. I was waiting and waiting and waiting for the end. I didn't know what to expect, and I tried to pray. I tried to believe in miracles again.

Maybe the doctors were wrong. Maybe we could keep this one, this one time. Maybe God would show up and change this for us. "Please?" was my constant soul-prayer refrain.

Please, please, please, please.

I talked to the baby every moment, willing him (because by now I was sure it was a boy, you see) to hold on, praying I could keep him. But I knew we wouldn't; somehow, I knew it was already over. This sorrow wasn't only about this one baby—not really: it was about all of our never-held babies, all of the mess of life, all of my doubts and fears and questions, all of it pressing on my womb in those days of waiting.

I stood in the streets of Bonn and asked God if he had forgotten me, if he had forgotten us.

There was no answer.

We slept in hostels and tiny pensions for those two weeks. After

I stood in the streets of Bonn and asked God if he had forgotten me, if he had forgotten us.

busy days of running around, organizing open-air meetings, driving the autobahn at white-knuckle speeds, getting to know our German and American hosts, listening to my husband preach through interpreters, and hosting barbecues, we would settle all the teens into their rooms and retreat to our Spartan quarters. We clung to each other in the darkness, not talking, tired, scared, waiting. There were no words left now.

Two days after we arrived home to our childless Texas rancher, labor started. I rocked on my hands and knees in our living room, Brian rubbing my back; we were scared and alone, ill prepared. We had our baby, together, just us two. Our suitcases weren't put away yet when we held our baby's teeny tiny body and finally surrendered.

The next Sunday, I felt empty and invisible, and the suitcases were still in the corner of our room when I reluctantly went to church. The sanctuary was crowded and loud, especially near the stage where I remained seated after the dismissal. I looked up, and I saw Pastor Kathleen looking at me very intently.

The former pastor and co-founder of our church, she was back for a visit with her family. We didn't know each other well because Brian had been hired after she had left for her new work, but we were acquainted because we saw her every time she came through town to visit. I always felt drawn to her somehow, but we never really talked. But that Sunday, I could see she had me in her sights. She crossed the auditorium; she crouched close to me, her face close to mine. She held my hands in hers and, without preamble, whispered that she felt that God had told her something about me, and she wanted to share it. I shrugged. Hadn't God forgotten me? I was unconvinced.

"I looked across the room at you, and God showed me that

"He wants me to tell you that *you are not forgotten.*"

your heart is broken, and you are weary." She lifted my chin and looked me straight in the face. She meant it; I saw this belief, this white-hot knowing in her. "And he wants me to tell you that *you are not forgotten.*"

You are not forgotten.

She said, "Now you know, don't you? Why our God said, 'Can a mother forget her child? Even so I will never forget you'? Because even if mothers forget, God will never forget you—never." She wrapped her arms around me like a mother does, pulled me close to her and whispered again, "You are loved. You are not forgotten."

I rested my head on her shoulder; she spoke my benediction and release. That day I went home, put away the suitcases, and stood in our quiet house with a new soul refrain: *I am not forgotten, I am not forgotten, I am not forgotten.* Even now. He remembered me. I pulled out the moving boxes; we were going home to Canada.

Just a few months later, I was sitting in my doctor's office on our neighborhood's high street, staring at her in disbelief as she said, "You're due in August. And everything looks fine."

After Anne was born healthy and strong, I was weak with relief and wonder. I sat beside my mother, holding our tiny Anne-girl to my own mouth, and I was crying into her downy hair. "I love her so much," I blubbered. "I kiss every centimeter of her; I love this part behind her ears, and her little mouth looks like a triangle—look at the little point at the top of her lips. And I can kiss that fold in her thighs and her armpits, and I want to lick the tears off her face. She's so beautiful, and she's really here, Mum; she's here for real."

I grew up always knowing the story I told you earlier, of how my mother was drawn to God through my birth, how her great love for her daughters put her feet on the path toward the empty tomb and the risen Christ and his invitation to recover her true life. It was my family narrative. But now it was my narrative, too, because now I understood. And because of the joy made deeper by suffering, my own soul was hungry for meaning and purpose and wisdom. I needed to know how to mother; I needed to know how to love while my heart was walking around outside of my body.[3]

This was my time.

It happens differently for everyone—for some, it comes through their work or through a relationship, through study or nature, through miracles or suffering. I do not think that my way is the only way or the best way; I know that not every mother receives the gift of children in this way or experiences loss as we did.

But the truth remains: regardless of the circumstances

unique to us, the voice of God has a habit of breaking through the noise of our lives, giving us a turning point, an epoch, so that we mark the rest of our lives differently from that moment on.

When we talk about these moments in our lives, we begin our stories with the words, "And then everything changed."

This was the point of healing for me: God used motherhood to save me all over again, *and then everything changed.*

Despite my great love for my tinies, I ran out of my own strength so quickly. I did not have the wisdom, let alone the patience, to parent three energetic tinies in a way that reflected God's heart back to them. I wanted to clear the path to God for them; I wanted to be an open door instead of a stumbling block to their understanding of the Abba I loved so deeply. We experienced another loss between the births of Anne and Joseph, and then, finally, our Evelynn Joan. And I couldn't do this in my own strength. When I tried to meet some impossible standard for motherhood, tried to earn my way to a weird sort of Proverbs 31 Woman Club, I collapsed in exhaustion and simmering anger, sadness, and failure. This was not life in the Vine, this exhausting job description; this was not the Kingdom of God, let alone a redeemed woman living full. This was the shell of someone trying to measure up, trying to earn through her mothering what God had already freely given. This was someone feeling the weight of unmet expectations from the Church and her own self and the world all at once.

In those days, my Abba gave me a glimpse—just a

glimpse—of his great unconditional love for us through my love for my own tinies. After that, I could not see him the same anymore. He wasn't in the fire or in the hurricane or in the earthquake; he was in the still, small voice—the creaking of my rocking chair in the wee hours of the morning, and the daily practices even in the never-forgotten lines from the old praise chorus "As the deer panteth for the water, so my soul longeth after thee" on my lips, sleeping milk-drunk babies, one after another, in my arms. He was in the sacred every-day of my life, redeeming it all, teaching me to pray, filling me with joy in my weakness, teaching me to rely on him. Here, I learned how I am more than my daily work, and yet he kept showing up in the mundane.

I remember one night in the wintertime. I stood in the middle of my living room, alone, after settling our youngest, Evelynn Joan, down again, our cold and dark house only lit with stars and streetlights. I couldn't go back to bed somehow; it was so quiet, so otherworldly.

I suppose every mother with a houseful of noisy children cherishes the rare quiet, but in this midnight hour, I was brimming with expectation in the loneliness. I could see the stars, and something in me wanted to stay there, awake with all the other mother hearts, up in the small hours; I felt them. I remembered a phrase from the Book of Common Prayer; I was with those who "work, or watch, or weep in the night," I prayed, and "give thine angels charge over those who sleep." Tend the sick, Lord Christ; give rest to the weary, bless the dying, soothe the suffering, pity the afflicted, shield the joy-ous; and all for thy love's sake. Amen."[4] A thin connection was there; I felt a holy sorrow and knowing, an enveloping love. I felt held, and I felt like I was holding. I was breathing in the Holy Spirit, cold and bright and enough. Two hours later, I wasn't so sanguine. I was tired and just wanted to sleep for two hours. I was muttering and resentful.

But as I lifted Evelynn, whimpering and longing and alone, again, she exhaled with relief, and she fell asleep minutes later, her tiny tummy full and her heart peaceful at my breast. If I were writing a story of my life in these nights, then it would be a chapter of metaphors.

This is what mothering taught me about God: we relax into this relationship.[5] He caught me with a taste of unconditional love, and then he taught me how to relax into that loving. He gently mentored me in eschewing perfor-mance and impossible obligations and outsider standards of success in favor of freedom and cre-ativity. Living loved, we relax our expectations, our efforts, our strivings, our rules, our spine, our breath, our plans, our job descriptions and checklists; we step off the treadmill of the world and the treadmill of religious performance. We are not the authors of our redemption. No, God is at work, and his love for us is boundless and deep, wide and high, beyond all comprehension. He remains faithful.[6]

> **This is what mothering taught me about God: we relax into this relationship.**

He is the Father in the story of the prodigal son, the one who watches the road every day for the first glimpse of dust moving, and he is the one who catches up his robes and runs headlong; he won't be held back, his sandaled feet pounding down that road to capture his son, his daughter, right into his arms again. And he covers over our protestations and our apologies with kisses and tears and welcome. Before we know it, we're having a party and dancing with our celebrating dad, clean, fed, secure, confident, loved as always for always.

You are not forgotten. Your story has not been forgotten; your heart cry has not been forgotten. Your sisters are not forgotten, and glorious times are ahead because "this resurrection life you received from God is not a timid, grave-tending life. It's adventurously expectant, greeting God with a childlike, 'What's next, Papa?' God's Spirit touches our spirits and confirms who we really are. We know who he is, and we know who we are: Father and children. And we know we are going to get what's coming to us—an unbelievable inheritance!"[7]

IF MORE MOTHERS were pastors or preachers, we would likely have a lot more sermons and books about the metaphors of birth and pregnancy connecting us to the story of God. I am rather tired of sports and war metaphors. If more mothers were pastors or preachers, perhaps the beautiful crèche scenes of Christmas wouldn't be quite so immaculate. We wouldn't sing songs of babies who don't cry. And maybe we wouldn't mistake quiet for peace.

As it is, we take on a properly antiseptic and churchy view of birth, arranged as high art to convey the seriousness and sacredness of the incarnation. It is as though the truth of birth is too secular for Immanuel. Birth doesn't look like our concept of "holy" in its real state.

So we think the first days of the God-with-us require the dignity afforded by our careful editing.

But the whole story of birth—this creating out of passion and love, the carrying of an ever-increasing beloved burden, the seemingly never-ending waiting, the knitting together of wonder in secret places, the under-the-surface fear, the pain, the labor, the blurring of that line between joy and "someone please make it stop," the "I can't do it" even while locked in the midst of the doing, the delivery of new life in blood and hope and humanity—this is the stuff of God.

There is something godly in the waiting, in the mystery, in the fact that we are a part of it—a partner with it but not the authors of it. You know that there is a new life coming, and the anticipation is sometimes exciting, other times exhausting and never ending. There is a price to pay for the privilege of life.

I was fortunate to give birth to two of our three tinies without complications. I find myself thinking of those experiences often; they were turning points in my life. My eldest daughter, Anne, was born in the hospital in a fairly usual way. My littlest girl, Evelynn Joan, was born at home, in water, with midwives attending us, and it was a beautiful and redemptive experience.

But it's the birth of our son, Joseph Arthur, that stays with me in these winter months. His was an unintended, unattended birth in our building's underground parking garage while we were on our way to the hospital.

No, I'm not kidding.

After beginning labor at home, we progressed far faster than we could have anticipated after our eldest daughter's thirteen-hour labor. This was unprecedented for us, so Brian thought we had time to make it to the hospital just a few minutes away. I had four contractions on our way down the hall and in the elevator of our apartment building. My poor man half-carried, half-dragged me into the parking garage, now desperate for help. He leaned me up against a support pole and ran to the truck to pull it over to me.

We were on our own—no midwife, no doctor, not even in our own home with a clean floor. Instead, we were in a dirty garage filled with cars and the smell of gas and tires. My husband was scared; a lot of things could go wrong in this scenario, but he had the good sense to act like he was in control and knew what he was doing. We were surrounded by strangers—helpful, concerned strangers but *strangers* nonetheless—and they were witnessing me give birth. I can only be thankful that this was before everyone had a smartphone otherwise, it likely would have been live-tweeted on Twitter with the hashtag #OMG.

Obviously, none of this was in my carefully typed-out birth plan.

My body had taken over, and all we could do was surrender to that moment fully. Every muscle in my body was focused; my entire world had narrowed to that very moment. Birth was happening, and it was happening now—nothing else mattered. One kind woman bravely stepped forward to kneel at my feet, just in case.

Beside our old Chevy TrailBlazer, standing up, with Brian's arms under my arms as a support, our son was born into my own hands, nearly nine pounds of shrieking boy-child humanity, welcomed by my hysterical laughter and his father's uncontrollable tears of relief. A few people applauded while they spoke to the 911 dispatcher.

> **I can assure you: there isn't anything very dignified about giving birth.**

I can assure you: there isn't anything very dignified about giving birth.

And yet, that was the moment when I felt my carefully constructed line between the sacred and the secular shatter once and for all. The sacred and holy moments of a life are often our most raw, our most human moments, aren't they?

I could preach on a street corner for days about the metaphors of birth and surrender. I could write pages of poetry for the braided strength of pain and creation and surrender, of the potency of loving.

But we keep it quiet, the mess of the incarnation—particularly at Christmas—because it's just not churchy enough, and many don't quite understand. It's personal, private, and there just aren't words for it—and it's a bit *too much*. It's too much pain, too much waiting, too much humanity, too much God, too much work, too much joy or sorrow, too much love, and far too messy with too little control.

And sometimes it does not go the way we thought it was supposed to go, and then we are left with questions, with deep sadness, empty arms after all of the waiting—with sadness unto death for the longing of a life.

My entire concept of God shifted through the experiences of pregnancy, loss, carrying babies, birth—all of it left my brain and my life and my theology to catch up with what my soul now knew deep in the center: God as Abba. I caught a glimpse behind the veil of his Father-Mother heart, and I drank deep. No theologian or countercircumstance experience can take away what I know, what many mothers the world over know in their heart of hearts about loss, sacrifice, pain, and birth, raising babies to life, and real transformation: it is Love, and it is sacred in its very messy living out.

There is a story on your lips, isn't there, Mama? Of how you saw the face of God in the midst of fear or pain or joy, and how you understood—really understood—the Mother Mary. She wasn't kneeling chastely beside a clean manger, refraining from touching her babe just moments after birth. Instead, sore and exhilarated, she likely pressed a sleepy, wrinkled, vernix-slick newborn to her mouth for kissing, treasuring every moment in her heart, marveling not only at his very presence but at her own strength. She knew that surrender and letting go and obedience are true work, and she tucked every baby mew into her own marrow.

Here, Son of Man, Son of God, is your mother's breast; find comfort, young star.

Paul wrote to the believers in Rome that we are a pregnant creation, hardly able to wait for what is coming next.

> The difficult times of pain throughout the world are simply birth pangs. But it's not only around us; it's *within* us. . . . We're also feeling the birth pangs. These sterile and barren bodies of ours are yearning for full deliverance. That is why waiting does not diminish us, any more than waiting diminishes a pregnant mother. We are enlarged in the waiting. We, of course, don't see what is enlarging us. But the longer we wait, the larger we become, and the more joyful our expectancy. Meanwhile, the moment we get tired in the waiting, God's Spirit is right alongside helping us along.[8]

This is part of what I mean when I talk about welcoming and affirming the stories of women. Paul understood and welcomed this, using metaphors unique to a woman's experience for his letters. For instance, mothers can tell *this* part of the

God story, the life lived in the in-between. There are so many stories in our churches—and I am not so proud and ridiculous as to think I am unique or that birth is the only experience that brings this kind of transcendent change. We can all testify to how God met us in our lives.

God put on flesh and blood through birth, now showing us what it means to be truly human. This is why I love testimony time in church. It has fallen out of fashion, but there is power in telling the stories of how God broke through for each of us. Women can tell their stories, testify to God at work.

God incarnate, Word made flesh, born of a woman— surely it matters. And at the time of year when the storm clouds gather early in the evenings and the cold creeps down from the north, I try to remember that the incarnation of Immanuel, God with us, means God put on flesh and blood and moved into the neighborhood through birth, now showing us what it means to be truly human. He never shied away from our most piercingly human experiences—birth, pain, death, sickness—and so, can we not find him and his redemption ways there still?

*If there ever comes a time
when the women of the world come together
purely and simply for the benefit of mankind,
it will be a force such as the world has never known.*

Matthew Arnold

CHAPTER EIGHT

Reclaiming the Church Ladies

We could probably have a few laughs tonight, and I know just the topic: women's ministry. Oh yes—we could trade stories of women's ministry mishaps and disasters, tales of craft nights gone awry, bunk-bed confessions at cry-fest retreats. Some of it might be genuine laughter, but it might also be the kind of laughter that is actually hiding deep hurts and misunderstandings, jealousies and bitterness, anger, pride, and inadequacies, the feeling of being overlooked and misplaced.

I was only thirteen when I attended my first women's ministry event. It was a fashion show. Stop it—I see you laughing. (For a while there in the eighties and nineties, homemade fashion shows were a terrible amount of fun, weren't they?) One lady in our church Bedazzled flowers onto jersey-knit harem pants and loose-fitting T-shirts. This businesswoman wanted to show off her outfits, maybe sell a few, and so the youth group girls served as models. I folded my thrift-store jeans and flannel shirt, set them on top of my Doc Martens, and carefully selected one of the jewel-toned sparkle outfits. I paraded across the altar of the church, pausing, turning, and retreating, blinking caked-on blue shadow at the sparsely filled pews of mothers and grandmothers. Jocelyn was the prettiest of the bunch, and so she wore a black leotard instead—better to showcase the fake gold costume jewelry ("Twenty-five percent off with the purchase of a sparkle outfit"). That experience rather ruined the song "Our God is an Awesome God" for me—it was our modeling music. I tripped over my own feet on my way onstage.

Once I was married, I tried to make the women's ministry thing fit, but most of the time, it was just as ill fitting as that emerald-green sparkle outfit. First of all, it was hard to get there: I worked full-time, and it seemed that most women's ministry events met on weekdays. But every once in a while I came to the evening events, dutiful and obedient to my responsibilities. We usually sat at round tables of eight, painstakingly decorated, to fill out work sheets. Question time was a staring contest of awkward silences, punctuated with responses suitable for consumption by total strangers thrown together for two hours over tea. Sometimes there were craft nights. But even when I was finally the target demographic of most church ladies' ministries, a stay-at-home mom right in the thick of my life, tired with a never-ending pile of laundry, still I didn't fit.

Some of us have stories of how we tried to fit in. We showed up at the events, played by the rules, and left feeling just a bit emptier and isolated, like a square peg in a round hole of crafts and Tuesday-morning coffee. I stereotyped perms and panty hose and, sadly, easily dismissed our sisters as old-fashioned church ladies. And then the church ladies who loved to craft and hang out on a Tuesday morning together felt judged and dismissed.

> We showed up at the events, played by the rules, and left feeling just a bit emptier and isolated.

So I gave up attending these kinds of official meetings for a while. I felt bad about it at first, but I was already choking on cute things and crafty ideas. I didn't need another fashion show or makeup tutorial, another chance to fill in a blank in a Bible study with a pink flower on the cover. Besides, the world can give us cute cupcake designs and decorating tips, scrapbooking parties, and casserole recipes.

Women are hungry for authenticity and vulnerability, real community—not churchified life tips and tricks from lady magazines. These can be fun, even relationship building, but surely it's not the whole picture. Some of us are drowning in our lives because of our past or our present, others are suffocating under the weight of unmet expectations, and still others are dying of thirst for want of the cold water of a friend. So many of us didn't grow up with mothers or grandmothers, fathers or grandfathers who loved Jesus, and our hearts are sadly aware of our own weaknesses and inadequacies in the face of real needs in our own homes and around the world. We're burned out on Facebook; we're ready to learn community.

We need our gathering together to be the place of *detox* from the world—its values, its entertainment, its priorities, its skittered fears, its focus on appearances and materialism and consumerism. We endure a constant barrage of unrealistic and unattainable standards for women on a daily basis: from our looks to our productivity to our homes to our marriages to our income to our pace of life. We try so hard to be everything to everyone and never age past movie star while we do it all.

It used to feel like women's ministry was laser focused on one type of woman, one season of a woman's life. But the women of our churches are not all wives and mothers. Some of us work outside of the home for diverse reasons, some of us love Victorian flowers and others fancy a bit of a modern edge. Some women like to do crafts, other women want to go golfing.

One of my friends has a saying: "If it's not true in Darfur, it's not true here." He means if we can't preach it in every context, for every person, it's not really for everyone, and so then we should probably ask whether or not what we are preaching is actually the gospel.

And that's how many of us feel about the segregation of women into one slot: it's just not true for everyone. We're not all in the same season of life, we haven't all made the same choices, we don't have the same life experiences and backgrounds, and we don't have the same priorities and callings or hobbies. We've been grouped together by folk wisdom and our common anatomy, and yet we are all bearers of the image of God as women. So now what?

A lot of women keep coming back to the church lady groups. Sometimes it's because they get to hang out with their friends, and they like that kind of stuff, and I think that's great. I know I often showed up because my friends were there. But I kept coming back because the truth is, I wanted what the world could not give me.

I wanted Jesus, and I wanted women in my life who loved Jesus, too.

Isn't that it? We are seeking Jesus—we want to smell him on the skin of others, and we want to hear tell of his activity. We are seeking fellow travelers for this journey. We are hungry for true community, a place to tell our stories and listen, to love well, to learn how to have eyes to see and ears to hear. We want to be part of something

We want to be with other women who know and love and follow our Jesus.

amazing and real and lasting, something bigger than ourselves.

We want to be with other women who know and love and follow our Jesus. Somehow we know that we will love him better if we hear from others how much they love him, too.

Maybe we don't need segregated women's ministry anymore. Maybe the time for that kind of one-size-fits-all thing is over. That can be scary for some people because programs are easier to produce than lasting relationships, and sometimes they even facilitate their development. But if it's working, then that's okay, too.

I'm not really one for seven steps to anything. I think that the Holy Spirit is more active than we realize, longing to give us wisdom and ideas, insights and creativity for our own context and communities. That's part of why I think women's ministry isn't usually a lot of fun for most of us. It's a one-size-fits-all club. And if there is one thing that women know about one-size-fits-all, it's that one-size-fits-all usually doesn't fit anyone.

As more and more women get honest about church and community, changes start to come. One group of women I know gathered together every week to talk about real stuff: sex, longing, hope deferred, marriage, friendship, hunger, worship, prayer, local issues, global needs—all of it. They sang a lot of songs together, and I have to tell you that the quickest way to make me cry is to put me in a room full of women singing songs about Jesus. Every time, luv, every single time. Whew.

And other women read interesting books together. They would do small groups every once in a while. They got together during weekday mornings, but they also got together on a weeknight once a month, and almost all of those gatherings featured women from within their community sharing about the Holy Spirit's movement in their lives. A group of older women did Saturday-afternoon child care for single mothers in the church, and let me tell you, it was a hit. (They used to offer child care to women who stuck around for Bible studies and craft stuff, but someone finally told them that what most of these women really wanted was an afternoon to grab a cup of coffee with a friend or get groceries or just go home and sleep. So they did that instead.) Sometimes a few of them would get together and knit things for babies in the church, and a few others liked to cook meals for sick people. But the best thing about them all was this: they did hard things together.

I've watched these women stand together through divorce and loss, through infertility and death, through eating disorders and brave leaps of faith. I've been a part of communities and churches who have decided they will be women who love, and there is this undercurrent of purpose and commitment, like, "Hey, we don't have all the time in the world here to play safe little church club for ladies; we have a lot of loving to do right now, so let's get on that."

It's not perfect by any stretch, but it's pretty great.

It did not happen by accident. It was—as is almost always

the case—born of a core group of women gathering and wanting more than work sheets and obligations and stereotypes. So they started to show up for each other. It took hold in their community, and its tendrils reach across continents now.

They live their lives as an invitation: to the world and to each other. You are always invited to participate, and you are always invited to start something if you don't see it existing yet. Some of the women in the church like to go to a local pretrial center, just to hang out with the women there. Sometimes they teach classes in parenting or finance or nutrition; other times they just show up at suppertime to talk and pray with the incarcerated women awaiting trial. Another group of them head out with a local ministry that provides warm coats and meals to prostitutes in a rough area of town.

These church ladies don't like to stay inside the church.

One year, they decided to adopt a school in their neighborhood; there were a lot of kids enrolled there living below the poverty line. When Loretta, who organized community outreach, called the school board, they loved the plan— on one condition. They wanted the church to take on *four* schools. Several of the men in the church jumped on board, too: they prayed for the schools regularly, organized coat drives, volunteered in the schools, threw parties for the staff and the kids—they just keep showing up and loving their neighborhood kids.

Another story: my friend Tina was at a conference when she heard about soldiers from the Lord's Resistance Army terrorizing northern Uganda. Women had their lips, ears, noses, and even genitals severed from their bodies. Many of these women are now HIV positive, marginalized and ostracized from their own communities and families because the scars define them.

Tina was in her twenties then, the daughter of immigrants, and she could not bear to think of how these women had endured war, loss, torture, rape, and now, on top of that, were unable to provide for their families due to disfigurement. It was unacceptable to her. So she asked what she could do. And it turned out it was pretty simple. Tina now considers this story her inciting incident, the moment when she realized she didn't have to live vicariously through anyone else; she could do something here, herself.

Some of these women needed relatively straightforward surgeries to reconstruct their bodies. Tina thought, *Well, I'll try to raise the money for one surgery for one woman.*

Even though she could hardly run down the block if someone was chasing her, she organized a half marathon to benefit Watoto's Living Hope project to restore dignity to women of Uganda.[1] When she announced it to her friends, a few people laughed at her: "You? Run a half marathon?"

So it shocked her when people actually signed up, including a few guys, and by the time she was done chasing everyone around the racetrack, she had raised nearly $43,600 to pay for *more than a dozen* surgeries.

People sometimes ask me, "So how do we have a great

women's ministry?" I never know how to answer that question. I don't really think that's the point of church. The bigger question is about the women of our churches, isn't it?

I think you have a great women's ministry when the women of your community fall wildly in love with Jesus. Church ladies like this are the overflow of women who are empowered to lead, to challenge, to seek justice and love mercy, to follow Jesus to the ends of the earth like our church mothers and fathers of the past.

> **You have a great women's ministry when the women of your community fall wildly in love with Jesus.**

You have a great women's ministry when there is room for everyone. You have a great women's ministry when you have detoxed from the world's views and unattainable standards for women and begun to celebrate the everyday women of valor, sitting next to you, and when you encourage, affirm, and welcome the diversity of women—their lives, their voices, their experiences—to the community.

You have a great women's ministry when your women are ministering—to the world, to the church, to one another—pouring out freely the grace they have received, however God has gifted them, including cooking and crafts, strategy, and leadership.

I often think of the great Methodist open-air preacher John Wesley's mother, Susanna, who led so many to the Lord. Her son said, "Since God uses women in the conversion of sinners, who am I that I should withstand God?"[2] William Booth of the Salvation Army reported that his "best men were women."[3] In his book, *Life and Work on the Mission Field,* J. Herbert Kane wrote home that "the more difficult and dangerous the work, the higher the ratio of women to men." [4] Korean megachurch pastor Dr. David Yong-gi Cho is quoted as saying, "All the churches are so little! And all of them are holding back their women, not allowing them to do what God calls them to do. I've told them to release their women, but they insist that's not the problem. They ask me, 'What's the key to your church?' I tell them again, 'Release your women,' but they just don't hear me!"[5]

Just as some men serve God in business and others in the farmlands, some women serve God in missions, and others serve God in their kitchens. There is not one way to be a woman; there is not one way to do women's ministry. There is only loving and serving God, doing life together in the full expression of our unique selves. Make room for them all and give glory to God.

I like being with these kinds of women because they are following so close to Jesus, and that is contagious. It rarely looks very exciting; sometimes it's downright mundane. But day after day, these church ladies choose to love, to make peace, to wake up, show up, and do life to-

> Day after day, these church ladies choose to love, to make peace, to wake up, show up, and do life together.

gether. They love their husbands, love their children, love each other, love themselves, and are coming at last to love the whole world.

So here is what I see when we reclaim the church ladies: a woman loved and free is beautiful. She is laughing with her sisters, and together they are telling their stories, revealing their scars and wounds, the places where they don't have it figured out. They are nurturers, creating a haven where the young, the broken, the tenderhearted, and the at-risk can flourish.

These women are dancing and worshipping, hands high, faces tipped toward heaven, tears streaming. They are celebrating all shapes and sizes, talking frankly and respectfully about sexuality and body image, promising to stop calling themselves fat. They are saving babies tossed in rubbish heaps, rescuing child soldiers, supporting mamas trying to make ends meet halfway around the world, thinking of justice when they buy their daily coffee. They are fighting sex trafficking. They are pastoring and counseling. They are choosing life consistently, building hope, doing the hard work of transformation in themselves. They are shaking off the silence of shame and throwing open the prison doors of physical and sexual abuse, addictions, eating disorders, and suicidal depression. Poverty and despair are being unlocked—these women know there are many hands helping turn that key.

There isn't much complaining about husbands and chores, cattiness, or jealousy when a woman knows she is loved for her true self. She is lit up with something bigger than what the world offers, refusing to be intimidated into silence or despair.

Oh, gracious—yes, it's a risk, and these women are often hurt. We screw up and become frustrated and angry with others, with our brothers, our husbands, our fathers, with our own selves.

But the gift of being vulnerable is something we are trying to give to our daughters, to the young and old women around us. We are creating a world where every woman can be who she is, without apology, in freedom.

She is loved. She is rising. She is awake at last, and as the Chinese proverb says, when sleeping women wake, mountains move. She is secure in the love and freedom of her God; she knows the voice of Jesus down in her bones. And therefore, she loves.

And this Love, Love, Love—stronger than death, stronger than evil, down to the depths and a new day dawning, to the corners where the devil is cowering and holding souls hostage, to the mountains for loud singing—is rising up.

These "typical" women, the ones we can dismiss or disqualify, are doing more to change the world than almost anyone else I've ever known in real life, because they are loving in every corner.

So don't look now, but sparks are flying upward from our fire. Maybe one will catch in your own heart.

I want to be with women like this. Let's reclaim the church ladies now. Church ladies aren't supposed to be kept in their women's ministry corner: sometimes they are ordained in our pulpits, other times they are working in human resources or scrubbing their floors, sometimes they are all of the above; they have a seat at the table and a soapbox on the corner, a pot on the stove, maybe a child on their hip. It's a lovely thing to watch men and women working together for the Kingdom of God.

> **It's a lovely thing to watch men and women working together for the Kingdom of God.**

Women have more to offer the church than mad decorating skills or craft nights. I look around: I see women who can offer strategic leadership, wisdom, counsel, and teaching. Their whole lives are an offering, and sometimes, the best way to properly celebrate that offering is with a dozen cupcakes and a fashion show, and that's okay, too.

The Spirit of God, the Master,
is on me because God anointed me.
He sent me to preach good news to the poor,
heal the heartbroken,
Announce freedom to all captives,
pardon all prisoners.
God sent me to announce the year of his grace—
a celebration of God's destruction of our enemies—
and to comfort all who mourn,
To care for the needs of all who mourn in Zion,
give them bouquets of roses instead of ashes,
Messages of joy instead of news of doom,
a praising heart instead of a languid spirit.
Rename them "Oaks of Righteousness"
planted by God to display his glory.
They'll rebuild the old ruins,
raise a new city out of the wreckage.
They'll start over on the ruined cities,
take the rubble left behind and make it new.

Isaiah 61:1–7 (excerpt; MSG)

CHAPTER NINE

Moving Mountains One Stone at a Time

(Please note that this chapter contains
stories of physical and sexual abuse.
Please read with discretion.)

Pastor Gaetan and his wife, Madame, had a dream for their little family of orphans: a real school. Their compound in Haiti was large enough to accommodate a school, but there was a large rocky hill in the middle, making it unsuitable for development.

One day, a skinny Haitian man in his sixties showed up with a pickax and a shovel. With the promise of only lunch as his daily payment, he shouldered into that stone and dismantled an entire rock hillside, shovel by shovel, in the equatorial heat. Later, we asked him why he felt compelled to do this, what motivated this tremendous effort, and he told a story of always longing to go to school; and even though it was too late for him, it was not too late for Haiti. It took months of hard labor, but he leveled that hill with his own wiry arms and strong back, and they set up their tent school: more than 150 kids from the neighborhood showed up in little brown uniforms, many girls among them.

> **Thanks be to God for men and women who pick up the stones, one after another, after another, until the mountain moves.**

Thanks be to God who moves mountains. And thanks be to God for men and women who pick up the stones, one after another, after another, until the mountain moves.

My life has not required a lot of miracles. This is no secret. My mother carefully curled my hair every week, and she tucked my sister and me into our matching white twin beds, her bedtime skin smelling of Noxzema. We went for family bike rides, and my dad flooded our Regina backyard one winter so I could learn to ice skate. We were brought up in the fear and admonition of Don Cherry on *Hockey Night in Canada*. We went to the doctor when we were sick, sure, but my dad also put his freckled hands on the tops of our heads and prayed healing into us. I have my own quiet sorrows, of course, but they are mostly common sorrows; and joy, especially the everyday quiet joy of loving and being deeply loved, has been mine in abundance.

When I was eighteen years old, far away from home, sitting in my university's chapel, I heard a story about a girl in juvenile detention who decided to follow Jesus after a lifetime of horrific abuse. Every person who should have loved her or, at the very least, protected her had viciously abused her—physically and sexually. She showed up at a church after her release from juvenile detention because a Christian staff member of the facility where she was incarcerated had assured her that if she went to church, she would find water for her thirsty soul, help, and a new family. Instead, just days later, her mother found her swinging from the light fixture, dead by her own hand. There was a note tucked in her jeans pocket, and she wrote of her despair and hopelessness, about how she went to church and everyone there was mean to her because she wasn't in the right clothes, she didn't own a dress, her haircut was blunt, she didn't speak the right language, and she wasn't pretty.

The last line of her suicide note read, "Mom, please bury me in my jeans."

The speaker during chapel that day was Nancy Alcorn, the former juvenile detention staff member who told that girl to go to church. Eventually she started Mercy Ministries, a nonprofit, free-of-charge residential home for young women longing for life and hope. Hers is a ministry that moves mountains one stone at a time. On the day I heard her speak for the first time, she told that story. I was the darling of loving parents, and my brain was struggling to keep up with this horrible thing. For I believed then, as I know now, that we are meant for love. My stomach was heaving and my eyes were stinging and I couldn't breathe. In just that one chapel service, in that one divine connection, God tuned the frequency of my heart to a new wavelength—to his heartbeat. I had no idea at the time how common that story was, let alone the severity of the situation for God's daughters all over the world. But I said my first *yes* to his heartbeat, the one that thumped under my rib cage. I knew Jesus, and I knew he loved us and wanted us all to be whole.

Years later, I volunteered with Mercy Ministries of Canada, and then I worked there for a few years. I always felt inadequate for the task yet strangely privileged. I was part of the marketing, communications, and development team, raising money so these young women struggling with drug and alcohol addictions, physical and sexual abuse, unplanned pregnancies, eating disorders, self-harm and mutilation, and trafficking could live at that home for free, just to experience God's life-transforming love and power. Miracles are happening right now, today—did you know?

Arrival day for a new girl was always hard. As she dropped her bags and stood, sometimes defiant, sometimes beaten, in her brokenness, guarded, I always wondered, *Is this enough? Are we enough?* And the answer was no; we weren't enough—

not always. But Abba is always, always, always enough for us all.

At our Christmas party a few years ago, Janelle held my baby in her arms while I drank punch and sang carols.[1] Like many of our girls who experience failed pregnancies, she was drawn to hold the babies of our staff members. A few months later, the first words out of her mouth at her graduation were of forgiveness. She wanted to make sure that we—all of us— knew that she had forgiven every single person associated with her story. And you can't un-hear her story—that bell will go on ringing in your ears because you can't, won't ever, forget that this beautiful young woman speaking of forgiveness was brutally raped by her father when she was three years old. Three years old. And he trafficked her for sex throughout her childhood—her *childhood*, the years when I was reading *Anne of Green Gables* and having my hair curled. She endured prostitution, mental health battles, anorexia, brutal repeated rapes, night terrors, loneliness, rejection. She came to us at Mercy, and not a single moment of the battle for her life was easy for her or for us. But here, now, was a miracle.

Recently, I visited Haiti with an organization called Help One Now, a tribe of individuals and churches committed to caring for orphans and vulnerable children by empowering and resourcing local leaders on the ground for community development. We met local leaders engaged in the hard work of rebuilding after the earthquake. In one of our meetings, local pastor St. Cyr informed us that Haiti was not moving forward even before the earthquake hit; and now the devastation had fully exposed Haiti's nakedness before the world.

During my time in Haiti and afterward, I have been a small part of these hard discussions about relief, international development, aid work, orphan care and prevention—all of the gigantic snarl of issues and mess and problems. I learned how vulnerable Haitian children are, particularly orphans, to being trafficked as slaves. The Haitian leaders talked soberly about how children are stolen, loaded up, and driven over the borders or to the ports, and then they are gone. I could not bear to think of this evil.

On that day, though, we were beside a cheerful church in the home of Richard, a local artist who created his own business based on a microfinance loan. Now his work is shown in galleries, and he provides for his son's schooling and care; and with his own money, he builds homes for other families. Economic justice is empowering; I saw Richard, and I think Richard and his son matter.

When we visited the makeshift tent city, I was angry. Oh yes—angry with God, angry with the world, angry with my own self. *How is this place even possible in our world?* I could not bear the smell, the sights, the truth of the place, and I saw babies the age of my tinies there. One small girl in a pink oversized men's dress shirt was steadily sweeping the dirt floor of her shack in a futile effort to keep their home neat and tidy, and all of my carefully reasoned understandings about how *everyone has a different calling* and *some of us are just called to different things than poverty relief and caring for orphans* stank rank like heresy.

I walked the rubble and nodded my gentle French Canadian *bonsoir* to their Creole *bonswa* as dusk gathered, and suddenly a thought broke into my mind: I would be terrified here. I would be so scared in the darkness. How did these women bear it? And one of our guides told me how before the United Nations installed spotlights it was literally a "rape camp."

And then we stood in that very same tent city, among our Haitian brothers and sisters, babies in our laps, and we sang the canvas roof off: "Glory, glory, glory to God; he's been good to us! Amen! Amen!" Me? I want to throw things when I am disappointed in my nice life. I pout, and I do not sing praise, because apparently, I expect my life to be perfect and clean and ideal and as pretty as Pinterest. I didn't want to cry in their church, out of respect, and so I sneaked my tears down my face. I still don't know if I was grieving or angry in that moment. A boy about seven years old asked me to marry him someday—such a flirt. There was a little girl in a blue dress covered with strawberries and trimmed in red gingham, her hair ribbons saucy

And then we stood in that very same tent city, among our Haitian brothers and sisters, babies in our laps, and we sang the canvas roof off: "Glory, glory, glory to God; he's been good to us!"

and alert; I want to remember her sweet and clean little dress there in the tent city always.

I think I got born again, all over again, that night, and now God smells like sweat, like open sewage ditches, like charcoal and avocados in addition to my northern lakes and pine trees, clean air, and water.

I had no frame of reference for Haiti. I still have no simile, no metaphor, but I saw God in Haiti—I did. He just didn't look the same anymore.

I met many men and women who will be famous in heaven. Through Pastor Gaetan and his wife, Madame—the couple I told you about earlier—I learned that faith can, in fact, move mountains. And this is where I learned that sometimes our most holy mountain-moving faith looks more like spending our whole lives *making* that mountain move, rock by rock, pebble by pebble, unsexy day after daily day, casting the mountain to the sea stone by stone rather than watching a mountain suddenly rise up and cast itself.

There were fourteen orphans living in tents on their property a few years ago. There was no clean water, no food, no school, but there was safety at the very least. Pastor and Madame, with their own two babies, took in all of these children to keep them safe from the streets, even if they could not provide for them. Every night, Pastor slept outside on a hospital cot among them, in the tents, in that insufferable heat, instead of his own bed. When I asked him why he did that, he looked straight at me—there may have been pity in his eyes—and he said, "A shepherd will not leave his little flock."

Americans, Canadians, Europeans, churches, mission agencies, nongovernmental organizations, all came to visit this makeshift family. They made him promises, and then they left, and nothing changed. And still Pastor and Madame stayed faithful to these little ones, going without to provide for them.

When the earth shook in Haiti, Pastor Gaetan lost his brother and many members of their congregation. Sixteen more orphans arrived on their doorstep. Thirty sad-eyed children, and only Pastor and his small family were there with them.

What was there to do, he said, but open their doors?

It took the entire day, every day in those days, to find water; food was an every-other-day-perhaps luxury, and they grieved and survived and worked and dreamed and worshipped and kept body and soul together . . . somehow. I don't know how, really.

Chris Marlow and the rest of Help One Now decided to work with Pastor Gaetan, and just two short years later, I stood in their humble home—yes, *home*—and I saw the stark beds where the children sleep, and I saw the well of clean water, and I saw beautiful, healthy children.

The orphan crisis is directly related to the economic and social development of families, particularly women, worldwide. There are 440,000 orphans in Haiti alone, according to the United Nations Children's Fund (UNICEF)—and this crisis is snarled and complex.[2] But as the people of God, we have a choice: we either make excuses or we make the mountains move, one stone at a time, one after another after another. Radical faith looks a lot like faithfulness, and look at what God can do with that.

Here is something I've learned about miracles: Miracles sometimes look like a *kapow!* lightning-strike revelation; and sometimes miracles look like showing up for your counseling appointments. Sometimes miracles look like instant healing; and other times, miracles look like medication and patience and discipline. Sometimes it's the daily unsexy work of loving people and choosing justice, even if no one ever notices. But know this: God's heart for humanity is good news for the poor, comfort for the brokenhearted, and release for the captives. His favor has come, and he gives "a crown of beauty for ashes, a joyous blessing instead of mourning, festive praise instead of despair."[3]

I suppose I'm a bit too liberal with the word *miracle* for most theologians. But I can't think of another word to describe what I see in Janelle and all of our Mercy girls, in our counselors, in our volunteers, in every single good and true church that welcomes our graduates into their lives like beloved daughters. I see miracles in every prayer we pray, every hand we hold, every word of hope and life we speak out, every eye we meet. I can't think of another word for the singing of "How Great Thou Art" in the middle of a tent city, for orphans finding families and community development efforts dedicated to keeping families intact, for the sight of a newborn baby girl nursing at the antenatal clinic under the watchful eye of midwives, for mountains moving and lonely children with perfect hair ribbons in a new school in Port-au-Prince, for women who have been abused rising up in strength to lead us all, for generative respectful friendships between the first world and the third.

Can't you see? It's all an act of protest, a snatching back from the darkness, a proclamation of freedom, a revolution of love. And isn't that a miracle?

It's been more than sixteen years since I sat in that chapel service, having my heart truly broken for the first time. Since then, it has broken repeatedly for God's daughters in our world, and it keeps being mended by the miracle of the everyday people of God doing the hard work of choosing love over fear, working out what God has already worked into them—moving mountains one stone at a time.

That's the thing when we say *yes* to God—it's not about that one *yes*. Our one *yes* keeps resounding and spreading, like ripples in a pond after a pebble is thrown into it, until the *yes* of God and the *yes* of our hearts and the *yes* of Jesus' love and the *yes* of us all sweep over the world.

Every year, I attend a gathering with women who love, these are my people. One year, I remember, a leader with the artistic eyes of a prophet handed out a spool of thick red thread and began to pass it down the rows. We wound that red thread throughout the room, all of us holding our little spot in the line, and it kept unfurling without end, like the ancient widow with her bottles of oil, until every woman in the room had a part of the red connection, the woman at the back connected to the one on stage, and we understood that we all matter.[4] If one of us tugged, we all felt it.

"Can't you see?" our prophetess said from the front. "If one of us is hurting, we are all hurting." She didn't mean just our little group there in western Canada; she meant all of us— we were holding you in our hearts and our sisters in Ontario, in Burundi, in Nebraska, in the Netherlands, in Melbourne.

During that day together, we laughed and cried; both came a bit more easily to us. We took turns getting up and telling the stories of how we are participating in God's movement in the world. We talked about scary steps, about the terrifying risks in community and generosity, of the shattering of our old comfort zones. It was one part reunion, one part commissioning: we didn't have time to be bickering and boundary drawing.

Janelle had graduated from the Mercy program by then, and she was at that gathering. She sat on a white couch at the front beside another graduate, Carissa, and Mercy Canada's executive director, Nicola. Janelle and Carissa were both there to tell their stories to us, Nicola was there to be with them, and we were there to receive their gift. As Janelle began to speak it out loud, even the glow of smartphone screens stilled. Some small red thread in my own heart unfurled and wrapped out around those two young women. I longed to hold them both while they spoke of their pain and brokenness. Stages don't feel right for testimony, do they?

Up on stage, Janelle suddenly stopped talking. Her voice crackled with pain; she couldn't say the next part of her story out loud. Her tongue wouldn't let her go, held with the pain of remembering. We sat in cathedral silence, and I was aching for her, up there, struggling, helpless to say her own words, wondering if we should go get her and let her step down.

Then, from just behind me, a woman's voice cried out in the waiting stillness. "It's all right, honey. We love you. We all love you. We've got you, sweetie."

"It's all right, honey. We love you. We all love you. We've got you, sweetie."

And that brave young woman up there, our hero, smiled through her tears as our voices grew louder. We were all saying it now, out loud, calling out of the darkness—*we love you, we love you, we love you, we love you*. Carissa and Nicola reached out to hold her hands, and then Janelle began to speak again, anchored by her sisters. She ground shame to a powder under her feet; she finished her story, brave, in her own voice, clearly proud of herself. We sobbed and clapped until our hands tingled.

The women in the room were a big reason those graduates were sitting on that couch. They had prayed for each of the girls, had given hundreds of thousands of dollars over the years for their home, for their certified counselors, and for food. These women have walked the property in prayer, dropped off bundles of clothes, preached the gospel with their lives to all of us. And as those two graduates stood on the stage, standing in for all of the girls in the home, all of the girls still waiting for a bed, all of the graduates worldwide, the women in the room welcomed Janelle and Carissa like daughters, like sisters, like they were the long-awaited child—for these girls we had prayed.

When I came home from Haiti, my friends and blog community participated in the fund-raising for a new school building with Pastor Gaetan at Yahve Shamma. It took a global village—men and women together—because this was church. We are the people, the men and women of God gathered together for communion and community and Holy Spirit breathing, just to scatter back out and set up another outpost of the Kingdom all over again.

In the face of oppression and darkness, the light is growing brighter, and we are on that side. We are among the hopeful men and women who love, and we are part of the redemptive movement of God in the world right now. Novelist Barbara Kingsolver writes, "The very least you can do in your life is figure out what you hope for. And the most you can do is live inside that hope. Not admire it from a distance but live right in it, under its roof."[5]

We were just a small group that day, one little gathering, when Janelle got up to talk. We were just a group of friends with a hunger to do something, to leave a legacy in Haiti by building a school. But we are not special—not really, just hopeful and determined. We represent a multitude all over the world; we're the men and women who have decided we will be the ones who love. Martin Luther King Jr. believed that almost always "the creative dedicated minority has made the world better."[6]

It's easy, perhaps, to forget that women are part of this mountain moving, but we have always been part of the great story God is writing. Today, right now, we are all working alongside preachers and teachers, activists and educators, mothers and fathers, farmers and entrepreneurs. We are in every corner of art and music, politics and the law, business, science, medicine, sports, technology, entertainment, academia. We may be underrepresented and underpaid, but we are here and we are there. We are moving mountains.

That's the beautiful thing about coming outside: you discover there are a lot of us already out here, waiting for you.

My friend Sarah is in Ottawa raising her two children, working alongside her husband on their law degrees because they have visions of economic development in the third world. Tara delivers babies in a midwifery clinic in Haiti; she's also the mother of seven kids. Kelley raises her children between two cultures while she contributes to Amahoro, which is an emerging African leaders network for theological conversation and to her African husband's community development in Burundi.[7] South African by birth, Canadian by marriage, my friend Idelette started a website called *SheLoves Magazine* as a gathering place for the everyday stories of the sisterhood at work in the Kingdom of God. Now SheLoves is a global movement.[8]

Jenn is bravely raising her son alone after her husband abandoned their family. Tracy leads worship ministries at church with her husband, their three little girls in the front row, watching their mama dance free on the stage, arms outstretched. Because of Tracy, my own daughters and son can dance in the aisle of church, free and alive in the presence of God and their community. Loretta prays at the pretrial center for women in custody. Rachelle counsels young women in crisis. Megan quit her long-cherished dream job to stay home and raise her baby son; there is a whole new dream job taking shape in her heart.

These women look just like you and me. Are you surprised?

Sometimes, by celebrating the evangelical heroes of the faith, we have inadvertently communicated something false: if it's not big and audacious and officially sanctioned, it's not good enough for God.

Brian and I jokingly refer to it as our Evangelical Hero Complex. All of those years of hearing sermons and reading books, going to youth camp and attending Bible studies—all those years of doing big things for a big God with big visions and big plans left us with crazy-high expectations for ourselves coupled with a narrow understanding of following Jesus. And when, like most of the kids of our tradition, we found ourselves in a rather usual sort of life, surprisingly *not* preaching to thousands on a weeknight, we were left feeling like failures, like somehow we weren't measuring up, we weren't serving God effectively. We must have missed it because isn't our life supposed to be about doing big, successful things for God with lots of attending attention and favor and audacious success?

It seems we've fixed a false hierarchy in our minds: everyone in public full-time vocational ministry is at the top of the Truly Committed Christian Food Chain, and the rest of us are support workers—some call us pew fodder. After all, if you are really serious about God, you go into full-time ministry.

And so we value the man preaching at the front to thousands more than the social worker with a caseload of seventy, more than the caregiver with one tired soul in her care, more than the single mother coaching basketball in the suburbs, more than the widow who knits for babies in the neonatal intensive care unit at the regional hospital.

We have been so busy celebrating the mythical evangelical heroes that we've forgotten that heroes come in all walks of life, callings, and success ratios. God marks a hero very differently than the world does.

God marks a hero very differently than the world does.

Here is the funny thing I learned when I began to disentangle from my Evangelical Hero Complex: I'm pretty sure that there aren't actually any big things for God.

There are only small things being done over and over with

great love, as Mother Teresa said. With great faith. With great obedience. With great joy or suffering or wrestling or forgiving on a daily basis, usually without appreciative applause or a slick video production summary. And grace covers all of it, and God makes something beautiful. One stone at a time.

I'm pretty sure that there aren't actually any big things for God. There are only small things being done over and over with great love.

It won't surprise anyone to know this: I am no hero. But I do want to take my life's work right now, today—whether it's a book I'm writing or a phone call I'm making or a meal I'm cooking—and I want to hold it all in my open hand with a Spirit-breathed prayer and intention. I want to be filled with the knowing that we are all a fragile universe needing love in this moment before I lay my gift on the altar and ask for holy fire to descend.

One soul is as important as ninety-nine, worth leaving everything behind to rescue. If there is one soul in your care, one face in your loving gaze, one hand in yours, then you are loving the world. As Wm. Paul Young writes, "If anything matters then everything matters," and so the work today, the love we give and receive and lavish on the seemingly small tasks and choices of our days can tip the scales of justice and mercy in our world.[9] Paul reminds us that we are a body, each part needed, each part necessary. There are different kinds of gifts, but the Spirit is the source of them all.[10] All of us, together, are Christ's body, and each of us is an important part.[11]

So, you might walk right past these women and never know that you were in the presence of world changers. It's likely you are already brushing shoulders with men and women of purpose and passion, the tribe choosing Love every moment, fighting back the darkness of despair, moving mountains stone by stone.

If we only had eyes to see
and ears to hear and wits to understand,
we would know that the Kingdom of God
in the sense of holiness, goodness, beauty is as close
as breathing and is crying out to be born both within
ourselves and within the world; we would know that the
Kingdom of God is what all of us hunger for above all
other things even when we don't know its name or realize
that it's what we're starving to death for. The Kingdom of
God is where our best dreams come from and our truest
prayers. We glimpse it at those moments when we find
ourselves being better than we are and wiser than we
know. We catch sight of it when at some moment of crisis
a strength seems to come to us that is greater than our
own strength. The Kingdom of God is where we belong.
It is home, and whether we realize it or not, I think we
are all of us homesick for it.

Frederick Buechner

CHAPTER TEN

Kingdom Come

The daughters of the earth are crying out for God's justice and peace. First world and third world and caught somewhere in between, we are buried in the world's power structures, tensions, histories, the old empire fallout of authority and patriarchy, war and economic injustice, hierarchy and systemic evils generation after generation. So as David Bosch beautifully explains it, we, the people of God, bravely "erect, in the here and now and in the teeth of those structures, signs of God's new world."[1]

I spent a year reading the Gospels during Brian's time in seminary. He was coming home with thick books about missional theology right at the time I was wondering why Jesus talked about "the Kingdom" so much and what in the world that meant. So together, we learned. (What can I say? We couldn't afford cable, and this is how we have fun.)

The Kingdom of God was the message of Jesus. As Dallas Willard points out, he proclaimed it, he manifested it, and he taught it.[2] The gospel is Jesus himself and his good news: *the kingdom has come.*

Thanks to winters on the Canadian prairie, I learned to walk in my father's footsteps. After a fresh snowfall, we would head outside, and in his big, old, white Sorels, my dad would lead the way through the deep snow. My sister and I carefully placed our feet into his footsteps to spare us the snow in our small boots and the attendant indignity of wet socks before the fun even began. We followed his path through the yard, across the field, and to the outdoor rink for yet another late-afternoon skate. Suppertime would come, and every Canadian kid will tell you there is no greater relief than the moment you take your skates off, and the feeling floods back to your frozen feet in a warm skate shack, and then you turn toward home in the darkness, walking deliberately in the footsteps of your father.

The Kingdom ways are a disciple's ways: we walk in the footsteps of our Jesus to learn how to be more like him, right now, in our own house, in our own jobs, in our own families, our churches, our communities, our world. We step into the holes in the snow ahead of us. We are apprenticed to the Master's ways, which means we try to live our lives the way Jesus would if he were in our place. We don't do this by effort: God does it through transformation. Once we become disciples of Jesus, we live in the Kingdom of God. And we cannot separate our salvation into a private event, divorced from what Darrell Guder calls the "advent of God's healing reign over all the world."[3] Ours is a distinct calling—to demonstrate the reality of God's redemptive power in the world today.[4]

According to R. Paul Stevens, a favorite professor of my husband in those years, mission is what "God is doing in the world through the church, and even without the church, to bring his creation to its consummation: unity and fullness in Jesus Christ."[5] We have been sent to the world as image bearers, emissaries of the Kingdom, much as the Father sent the Son; and as the Father and Son sent the Spirit, we are now the Sent.

And as David Bosch writes, to "participate in mission is to participate in the movement of God's love toward people, since God is a fountain of sending love."[6] The mission of God is your mission, and it's mine, and it's the work of every son and daughter living loved as we join with God in his great and gorgeous mission. Jesus feminism is only one strand of this glorious work.

The Kingdom of God stands in sharp contrast to the ways of the world. The Church has not and does not always stand in sharp contrast. But I have hope because we are not the only small fire here on the shore; we are one of many down through the ages. Yet the Kingdom of God is bigger even than the Church's failures and successes, disappointments, sell-outs, compromises, and grand triumphs.

The people of God have a unique and beautiful message for the women of the world: You are fearfully and wonderfully made. Your Abba delights in you. You are equal. You are lovely. You are called; you are chosen; you are beloved. You are gifted. You belong. You have worth and value. You matter.

Friend, we can leave this bonfire tonight, and together, we can post a few signs and arrows of direction to the Kingdom: *This Way to Narnia.*

Women—sisters, daughters, mothers, wives, friends—the Kingdom has come. God is your home. You will find rest for your weary soul. There is healing and forgiveness here. There is justice for the wrong done to you. There is dignity and honor.

What a wild idea—an exciting one, really. Imagine our churches and communities, our own lives as outposts of the Kingdom way of life, right where we are, right now. As Carolyn Custis James proclaims in (my very dog-eared copy of) *Half the Church,*

> The community of God's people should be the epicenter of human flourishing—where men and women are encouraged and supported in their efforts to develop and use the gifts God has given them wherever he stations them in his world. . . .

God never envisioned a world where his image bearers would do life in low gear or be encouraged to hold back, especially when suffering is rampant, people are lost, and there is so much kingdom work to do. He wants his daughters to thrive, mature, gain wisdom, hone their gifts, and contribute to his vast purposes in our world. . . . God created his daughters to be kingdom builders—to pay attention to what is happening around us, to take action and contribute.[7]

As we welcome and affirm the voices of women in our churches and communities, as we learn to walk in an attitude of trust instead of the language of combat, as we participate in God's redemptive movement for women, as we make space for one another's wisdom and experiences, as we care for the oppressed in tangible ways, we are joining with God in his caring, sustaining, and transforming activity on earth.[8] As J. C. Hoekendijk says, our role is to "find out what God is doing in the world, celebrate it and embrace his mission."[9]

The Kingdom of God won't be built or expanded, strategized and manufactured by our own efforts, however well meaning. That simply isn't the language of the New Testament. The Kingdom of God is much more beautiful than a sales program or marketing plan or government benchmark. The Kingdom of God works into us like yeast, and it grows like a seed in good soil. It enters quietly, holistically, radically, joyfully subversive, right into the core of our humanity, un-furling, renewing, and giving work to our hands. It shows up when we live loved and where we love each other well. And the Kingdom of God lasts.

As we follow Christ in the counsel of the Holy Spirit, rest-ing in the love of our Abba, we no longer fear—for there is no fear in love. We do not fear slippery slopes, we do not fear each other, we do not fear change, and we do not fear our own selves or what people can do to us. This fearless love allows the mission of God to infuse our smallest seed lives, growing through to our families, our communities, our culture, our government—tendrils twining. The root of the tree of Jesse is growing wild and beautiful.

The Kingdom of God is a pearl of great price. It's the yeast in homemade bread, rising only after a good thumping, warm and alive. It's the smallest seed of a shrub, and it's a mighty oak of righteousness. It's the treasure in the empty field; it's worth selling everything to own—your entertainment, your 401(k) or your registered retirement savings plan, your home, your comfort, the sand where you stick your head, your last word, your right answers, your safe and predictable nice little life centered on avoiding heartbreak or inconvenience to your schedule. It's a strong tower, a refuge. We aren't expanding or building this Kingdom—we are receiving; we are inheriting and participating. This is no branding brainstorm: this is the Kingdom of God, and it is already here. Taste and see.

Every good and perfect gift comes from our loving Father

of lights.[10] We catch glimpses of the Kingdom in these gifts. We practice the Kingdom like that old piano, exercising beauty and freedom and joy, fitting our footsteps into the footsteps of our Jesus. This is the way: walk in it.

I think the Kingdom is in every good and perfect moment in our lives, because these moments serve as a taste, just a small taste, of what God truly intends for us. It's in our bonfire for dancing and laughter. It's friends who show up when it matters. It's making your tinies laugh. It's sleeping babes curled into their mother's breast and the heft of holding another soul. It's wisdom and beauty, peace, love and joy, and then it's also good coffee and real food, late-afternoon sun and handmade quilts. It's the renewal of morning. It's making love and waking up in each other's arms, satiated and tangled.

The Kingdom is a glimpse of true manhood and womanhood, without fear or stereotypes or abuses from the world. We are the restored image bearers in concert together, all participating, all parts functioning with holy interdependence. It's trust and laughter and holy risk taking; it's vocation and work and worship. It's sharing leadership and responsibility. It's turning away from the language of hierarchy and power to the posture of servanthood. It's affirming all the seasons and callings of each other's lives. It's speaking out and working and advocating on behalf of our oppressed brothers and sisters around the world.

His is a Kingdom of inversions, of the least being the greatest. In this Kingdom, both the child and the aged are loved and respected. It's a gorgeous, crazy family that listens and talks too loud and loves you all the harder in your weakest moment. It's art and co-creation; it's music and theology in every daily rhythm of our lives. It's giving our money away, because there is a bigger treasure in the giving than in the hoarding. It's provision; it's enough. It's a welcome. You—yes, you—are welcome here. We've been waiting for you.

The Kingdom is an about-face to the world's ways. It is eyes that see and ears that hear and hearts that understand. It's a mountaintop moment of inspiration, and it's the mystery of finding God in the smallest and most mundane of moments. It's diverse and global, a song of reconciliation.

The Kingdom is an about-face to the world's ways.

The voiceless are given a song, and the rest of us finally listen to what they have been saying all along. The tired receive new strength in joy. In the Kingdom of God, there is no such thing as an outsider.

It is ropes dangling from old branches for us to swing out and drop into the depths of that delicious space between delight and fear of the unknown, like children swinging into a lazy spring-fed river. It is every sin, committed in thought and word and deed, forgiven, cast as far as the east is from the west.

And I also think the Kingdom is every evil and terrible moment in a life somehow redeemed. It's restoring beauty to the night instead of remembrances of terror. Someday, when Christ returns and sets all things right, and heaven is established on earth, because as theologian N. T. Wright writes, "Jesus's resurrection is the beginning of God's new project not to snatch people away from earth to heaven but to colonize earth with the life of heaven. That, after all, is what the Lord's Prayer is about."[11] There will be no more tears, no more sorrow, no more good-byes. The Kingdom will be a reunion, a shocking and wild oh-hallelujah-at-last gathering. The castoffs of our world—those whom our culture disdains and discards and disappoints and devastates—will lead the laughter and the dance. Part of our worship must be wiping the tears from every face, the labor of drawing buckets from the well of salvation to water the tired soil into renewal.

It is messages of joy and open gates to welcome our children coming home from war, their swords forgotten, assault rifles discarded. It's a rich harvest of exiles gathered from all the nations; it is weapons beaten into plowshares.

This is the world we are prophesying with our very lives.

Our Abba is steadily putting things right. He will not tire, he hasn't fallen asleep on the job, and he will not quit. He has not forgotten you. In the darkness, there are fires on the shore. God's glory will shine like the noonday sun. And no one will be lost. We will be the people of life, not death. And we're setting up an outpost of the Kingdom here on the shore.

SO WHAT DO we do as we seek to follow our Father's footsteps into the Kingdom? How do we set up those outposts? I think it begins with peace. The word for peace I'm thinking about here is the old Hebrew word, *shalom*. God's shalom is complete peace: wholeness, health, welfare, safety, soundness, tranquility, prosperity, perfectness, fullness, rest, harmony. This peace is found in Christ and his Kingdom.

Shalom is not only a "cessation of hostilities," explains Darrell Guder in *Missional Church*. "Instead, shalom envisions the full prosperity of the people of God living under the covenant of God's demanding care and compassionate rule. In the prophetic vision, peace such as this comes hand in hand with justice. Without justice, there can be no real peace, and without peace, no real justice. Indeed, only in a social world full of a peace grounded in justice can there come the full expression of joy and celebration."[12]

Shalom is an active word; we are to seek shalom, make space for shalom, pursue the path of shalom precisely because the Way of Jesus is the way of shalom, and we are the People of Shalom. It's a way of paying debts, setting the world right, restoring balance. When we are in right relationship with Jesus, then we are in right relationship with one another, even with our own selves.

God hungers for justice. And as his people, we hunger for justice. It is precisely because of our great love for God that we pursue justice, make peace, love our enemies, seek to reconcile souls to their Savior, care for widows and orphans, build schools for kids halfway around the world—and also make supper and check homework every night for our own tinies.

We reject the lies of inequality, we affirm the Spirit, we forgive radically, we advocate for love and demonstrate it by folding laundry, and we live these Kingdom ways of shalom prophetically in the world.

Many of the seminal social issues of our time—poverty, lack of education, human trafficking, war and torture, domestic abuse—can track their way to our theology of, or beliefs about, women, which has its roots in what we believe about the nature, purposes, and character of God. Twenty-two thousand children die each day due to poverty. And they "die quietly in some of the poorest villages on earth, far removed from the scrutiny and conscience of the world." According to UNICEF, some 1.1 billion people in developing countries have inadequate access to water, and 2.6 billion lack basic sanitation.[13]

Women aged fifteen through forty-five are more likely to be maimed or die from male violence than from cancer, malaria, traffic accidents, and war combined. One-third of women face abuse at home.[14] Another major study found that in most countries, between 30 and 60 percent of women had experienced physical or sexual violence by a husband or a boyfriend. Up to 70 percent of female murder victims are killed by their male partners.[15]

> It is precisely because of our great love for God that we pursue justice, make peace, build schools for kids halfway around the world— and then make supper every night for our own tinies.

Over 135 million girls and women have undergone genital mutilation, and 2 million more girls are at risk each year. "Honor" killings, in which a woman's relative murders her for disgracing the family, are also a concern—a concern not limited to borders far away.

Women compose 70 percent of the world's poorest people and own only 1 percent of the titled land, according to a UN report.[16] They suffer from unequal access to education and training, as well as from discrimination by their employers. The majority of women earn (on average) about three-fourths of the pay that men receive for doing the same work, outside of the agricultural sector, in both developed and developing countries. Studies have indicated that when women hold assets or gain income, the money is more likely to be spent on nutrition, medicine, and housing; consequently, their children are healthier. For every dollar a woman earns, she invests eighty cents in her family. Men, on the other hand, invest around thirty cents and are more likely to squander money on alcohol and other vices. More than seventy-five million primary school–age children are not in school. More than half of these children are girls, and 75 percent of them live in sub-Saharan Africa and South Asia. Of all the primary school–age girls globally, 20 percent are not in school, compared to 16 percent of boys in this age group. That's one in five eligible girls worldwide who aren't going to primary school.[17]

And closer to home for many of us, official low estimates state that more than 300,000 women are raped every year in the United States.[18] Two small examples within media are the high fashion industry's images of sexualized violence against women for advertising purposes,[19] and the increasing pornification of our culture.[20] Anecdotally in the news recently, there are the high school football players at a house party who took photos of an unconscious girl before and after raping her,[21] and the comedians who joked about how funny it would be rape a woman in the audience.[22]

These statistics and anecdotes are what I think about when people ask me if we're past the need for feminism because behind each stat, there is a story and a soul and a consequence.

"Aslan is on the move," wrote C. S. Lewis in my dog-eared copy of *The Lion, the Witch and the Wardrobe*. Me? I want to move with our not-safe-but-good God.

I'm through wasting my time with debates about women-should-do-this and women-should-not-do-that boundaries. I'm out. What an adventure in missing the point. These are the small, small arguments about a small, small god.

Our big and good God is at work in the world, and we have been invited to participate fully—however God has gifted and equipped and called each of us. One needn't identify as a feminist to participate in the redemptive movement of God for women in the world. The gospel is more than enough. Of course it is! But as long as I know how important maternal health is to Haiti's future, and as long as I know that women are being abused and raped, as long as I know girls are being denied life itself through selective abortion, abandonment, and abuse, as long as brave little girls in Afghanistan are attacked with acid for the crime of going to school, and until being a Christian is synonymous with doing something about these things, you can also call me a feminist.[23]

Some people think that a redemptive movement hermeneutic is prideful, that it does not value Scripture. After all, won't this erode the infallibility of the Bible? Isn't it prideful to decide what Paul, for instance, *really* meant? Not at all! I believe this movement is scripturally supported and that it continues the movement of the Holy Spirit as given to the Church in Acts. But it also requires a healthy dose of humility and submission to Christ. Because now, as we read the Bible, it places a demand of action and thoughtfulness on us as we continue to carry the story of God forward into the twenty-first century.

American preacher and theologian Jonathan Edwards aptly said, "The task of every generation is to discover in which direction the Sovereign Redeemer is moving, then move in that direction."[24]

This requires us to prayerfully ask ourselves, Where is God moving? And how can I live out God's shalom?

What would it look like for us to prophetically live that into reality in our churches, to bring the Kingdom into our homes, our marriages, our everyday walking-around lives? Where is God moving, how is God already at work, and how can I join in? What is God's heart for humanity? And am I participating in making *that* vision a reality? What mountain stone am I moving in a radical act of faith?

It's a scary thing, a life-changing, paradigm-shifting thing, to honestly ask yourself this question: Am I moving with God to rescue, restore, and redeem humanity? Or am I clinging fast, eyeteeth clenched, to an imperfect world's habits and cultural customs, in full knowledge of injustice or imperfections, living at odds with God's dream for his daughters and sons? He calls his people farther and farther out into the fresh air for the wild and holy work of restoration, renewal, and redemption.

> It's a scary thing, a life-changing, paradigm-shifting thing, to honestly ask yourself this question: Am I moving with God to rescue, restore, and redeem humanity?

As Carolyn Custis James asks us, "Is Jesus' gospel merely a kinder, gentler version of the world's way of doing things, or does the gospel take us to a completely different, long-forgotten way of relating to one another as male and female?"[25]

Within this framework of living, we can no longer use a small handful of Scriptures taken out of their original context as an ongoing excuse to oppress or silence or subjugate women, however well intended and benevolent, however small and insignificant, however overwhelming and systemic.

My friend, we have lost our footing for that old world of patriarchy and proof-texting sours on our tongues in the face of injustice. Instead, we are participating now in the coming

Kingdom of God. We are on a mission together, men and women, joining in God's great rescue.

For the sake of the gospel, women must speak—and teach and minister and prophesy, too. For the sake of the gospel, a woman must be free to walk in her God-breathed self as the *ezer kenegdo* in whatever vocation and season and place of her life. And she does all of this alongside her brothers, as the *ezer* warrior of Creation's intent, to see God's Kingdom come and his expressed will done.

Misguided hierarchies and inequalities have no place in God's shalom. Patriarchy isn't the dream of the Kingdom of God, and so we can loosen our grip on this old culturally conditioned way of thinking, unfurl our fingers, and simply let it sink to the bottom at last.

Patriarchy will not allow us to participate in the restorative movement of the Spirit for women and men's intended alliance. Carolyn Custis James wisely observes, "When half the church holds back—whether by choice or because we have no choice—everybody loses and our mission suffers setbacks."[26]

Me? I can see the lights of that city on a hill growing bright, and it makes me want to fling open the doors. The Bridegroom is coming. *Can't you feel that?* In the ache and struggle and evil of our imperfect world, no wonder we long for the Kingdom of God's shalom right down to our marrow. The tears are pricking; my heart is beating; something is happening here: *Aslan is on the move.* God's dream is coming true, day by painful push-back-the-darkness day.

When it's over, I want to say: all my life
I was a bride married to amazement.
I was the bridegroom, taking the world into my arms.
When it is over, I don't want to wonder
if I have made of my life something particular, and real.
I don't want to find myself sighing and frightened,
or full of argument.
I don't want to end up simply having visited this world.

Mary Oliver, "When Death Comes"

CHAPTER ELEVEN

Intimate Insurgency

So where do we go from here?" you ask. "Now what?" the churches say in frustration. "How? What are our seven steps to equality? How do we make other people believe it? How do we change things for women in our church and in the world? What shall we do?"

I don't know.

(Isn't it funny how scared we are to admit that we don't know? It's as if we're supposed to have it all figured out before we begin.)

But I trust Him. I trust Him with every aspect of our life and our world, and I yearn to participate in his activity in the world. Jesus is building his Church, not only by constitutions and codes, but by shaping hearts and minds to his way of life. We are a family, not a firm, scattered and yet gathered.

Biblical equality is not the endgame; it is one of the means to God's big ending: all things redeemed, all things restored. Jesus feminism is only one thread in God's beautiful woven story of redemption.

Begin here: right at the feet of Jesus. Look to Love, and yes, our Jesus—he will guide you in your steps, one after another, in these small ways until you come at last to love the whole world.

I can't tell you your place in this story. No one can. And that is how God intended it: go to him. If any of us lack wisdom, we are to ask God—he is faithful to give it.[1]

I lack wisdom. Oh, the ways in which I lack wisdom! I lack wisdom in my daily walking-around life as a wife and a mother, as a writer, as a friend, as a daughter, as a disciple—let alone wisdom for the systemic patriarchal treatment of women in the Church as a whole, and the big questions of our age concerning injustices and evil toward women worldwide. I am one small mama warrior fighting in this war for women; I am not the Winston Churchill of this war (maybe you are, though . . . We should be so blessed). No, I'm more underground resistance, an intimate sort of insurgent. I think I'm one of many taking every opportunity, however small, to build a prophetic outpost for the Kingdom's way of womanhood.

It's in the small ops for me. The monthly check sent off

to the residential home for girls struggling with life-controlling issues. The determination to value my daughters and son for their intrinsic worth. The giving of respect and honor to the stories of women around the world—and in my neighborhood. The choosing of

I'm one of many taking every opportunity, however small, to build a prophetic outpost for the Kingdom's way of womanhood.

a church that affirms women in ministry in practice as well as on paper. The raising of my tinies to follow the example of Christ first. It's in the choices of everyday justice. It's in the refusal to ignore the hard stories—however much I want to stick my head in the sand and act like they're not happening. It's in the writing of the letter to a small girl in Rwanda who lost her parents to AIDS. It's in opening our homes with true hospitality and remembering the lonely. It's in using my words to love us all. It's in resolutions and votes in our churches. It's in the openness only born of the Spirit. It's in the following of the small and daily nudges from Abba until ours is a transformed life on the narrow path of the arc of God's redemptive movement, ever moving forward.

We are making space for God behind enemy lines because we are living here. We may be a people in exile, but we are planting gardens, working for the good of the city.

In the meantime, these small ops serve to dismantle from inside enemy lines, from inside our own hearts, from inside our daughters and sons, from our friends. And then it's by joining our hearts, our hands, our ears, our energies, our minds, and our voices to our sisters the world over. Maya Angelou writes, "Strictly speaking, one cannot legislate love, but what one can do is legislate fairness and justice. . . . Legislation affords us the chance to see if we might love each other."[2]

God's justice doesn't come without his presence. When we invite the presence of God into our lives, we then watch, watch, watch where he goes, and we simply follow.

Even in our activism, in our preaching-with-our-feet-and-voices-and-hands-and-money lives, we are not always given clear choices. Do we stay in this particular church or leave? Do we continue to argue for equality in this institution, or do we come outside of those tired over-and-over-again arguments? Do we stay in a marriage that does not glorify God, or do we leave? Should we abolish women's ministry or keep on planning retreats and conferences? Should you stay home with your children or go to work? Do you preach from a pulpit, or do you preach quietly in relationship? Do you pursue full-time vocational ministry or choose another path? Do you seek justice in the suburbs or move your family around the world? Do you set quotas for how many women are on your church board? Do you put your mind and energy behind meaningful change through political action and policy changes in the world?

These are not right-or-wrong, black-or-white, yes-or-no sorts of issues. These questions are only answered by abiding in the Vine, searching Scripture, taking wise counsel, praying, and then a bit of holy risk taking.

Sometimes it's easier to talk about the whole big, wide Church or the whole big, wide world than it is to talk about our own lives, isn't it?

We can pontificate for days on what the Church is doing wrong and what needs to change, casting judgment easily. We tend to think en masse or point fingers as a coping form of disassociation from our own culpability.

But Jesus was clear on this: renewal in your world starts in your own heart and life. We need to look to the plank in our own eyes long before we start straining at splinters in the eyes of others.

And perhaps we need to repent. Perhaps we need to forgive our oppressors, or our preachers, our politicians, and our own selves. Perhaps we need to seek reconciliation, but perhaps we need to open our hands and let it go. Perhaps we need to follow our Shepherd to the high places, step after step, trusting his active leading in each decision. Perhaps we need to change our tone or our tactic.

God may call you to lead the charge, or he may call you to a quiet life of profound consequence. God may call you to marriage or to singleness—likely a bit of both in your life. Either way, you are living loved, his burden is easy, his yoke is light, he gives joy for mourning, beauty for ashes, and our only responsibility is to follow in his footsteps.

Perhaps there is a place first for some honest questions,

starting maybe with your own small home, your own soul. We must root out the lies of the enemy from our thoughts about one another, from our marriages, from our churches.

God's type of revolution doesn't happen with swords or manipulations, with broken relationships and I'm-right-you're-wrong rhetoric. Even if we change practices or behaviors, we are seeking transformed hearts. We must know in our bones God's heart for equality and wholeness in the Body of Christ then live our lives out of that truth, with invitation and joy, as living prophets of God's way of life.

And pray. Oh, sisters and brothers, *pray*—go boldly to the throne of grace where we receive mercy for our sins. He is our Hope, our Resting Place. We can repent—such an old-fashioned word for simply turning around and stepping back into the footsteps of Jesus. Pray for your marriage, your children, for your church and your pastors. Pray for your friends and for your mentors and heroes, and your parents. Pray for women the world over, pray for world leaders, pray for prophets and poets and pragmatists and policy makers all to rise up in participation with God's shalom. Pray for wisdom in each decision, pray to hear the voice of God clearly as you subvert the world's ways of love and marriage, men and women, authority and submission, war and eye-for-an-eye versions of justice, and then pray with your feet.

We need the pragmatists and policy wonks, the ones committed to seeing God's way of life come to fruition through strategic planning, resolutions, government pressures, and elder boards. We also need the prophets and poets, singing us home, giving us a glimpse of the better way. We need institutional churches and misfit communities; we need Canada and we need Cambodia; we need all of us, a company of the redeemed, a glorious symphony instead of a pack of dislocated, dysfunctional soloists.

We need you: your voice rising, your hands working. You matter in this story.

This is why I speak so often about living loved first, above all else, because that is our starting point for our real life, whether our callings are as pragmatists or policy makers or prophets or poets, whether we are the highly visible change makers or the quiet subversives.

As Eugene Peterson paraphrases the words of the Apostle Paul, "We first take our everyday, ordinary life—our sleeping, eating, going-to-work life—and place it before God as an offering. Embracing what God does for us is the best thing we can do for him. When we fix our attention on God, we'll be changed from the inside out. We'll readily recognize what he wants from us and quickly respond to it. Unlike the culture around us, always dragging us down to its level of immaturity, God brings out the best in us, develops well-formed maturity."[3]

Unlike the culture around us, God brings out the best in us.

"If the disciples had set out to 'change the world,' they would have failed miserably, lost in their own ingenuity and wisdom to accomplish so large a task," writes Wayne Jacobsen.[4] Instead, Jesus admits he's called them to a large work, but he encourages the disciples: "Don't be overwhelmed by it. It's best to start small. Give a cool cup of water to someone who is thirsty, for instance. The smallest act of giving or receiving makes you a true apprentice. You won't lose out on a thing."[5]

Nothing changes in a true, God-lasting way when we use people or push agendas or make finger-pointing arguments or accusations of heresy. The justice we are seeking is God's justice—justice that leaves no one out, no one left behind. His justice breaks chains, rids the world of injustice, frees the oppressed, cancels debts. He's interested in seeing us share our food with the hungry, invite the homeless and poor into our lives, put clothes on the shivering ill-clad, and be fully present to our own families.[6]

As feminists, we've sometimes found that our self-efforts are misguided and often frustrating. We see injustice and want to overturn it—*now*. I get this, and I feel it, too. We absolutely need to engage in the daily, impossible, frustrating, swimming-upstream work of overturning injustice.

But we must remember that all of those efforts are ultimately frustrating, sometimes even misguided, *without Christ*. If Christ is not at the center of the work, if he is not the author of the work, the glory of the work, then it is often unfruitful and incomplete. We may win the battle of the moment, but the war of hearts and minds falls to the enemy, bitterness takes root, and the war continues on and on. Only Christ can pull out the root of the sin that started it all.

But when Christ begins a work, he finishes it. His heart is for his sons and daughters, for their freedom, and he welcomes them home to the family; we are part of that holy work. And if we are called to the hard, unsexy work of setting things right slowly with little visible success, we can remain joyful in perseverance. We must obey God, and our obedience to God may be perceived as rebellion and pride by some; others will see it as giving in or not giving enough.

The Kingdom of God is like a banquet. Everyone shows up looking for the seat of honor, longing for the head table. But Christ tells us to sit at the last place: "Then when the host comes he may very well say, 'Friend, come up to the front.' That will give the dinner guests something to talk about! What I'm saying is, If you walk around with your nose in the air, you're going to end up flat on your face. But if you're content to be simply yourself, you will become more than yourself."[7]

True justice and equality won't flow from celebrity or position or platform. Justice flows from the heart of our Abba, and when our hearts are tuned in to his heart, that justice flows through our own right-now lives.

We may occasionally find ourselves in a place of honor and influence, sure, but even if we do not find honor here in this world, we are still part of God's shalom outpost in the seed planting and tending we do to his glory. We can bear with our weaker brothers and sisters with grace and love, building them up in love.[8]

Gretchen Gaebelein Hull is a dedicated Christian feminist. She also understands this paradox of which I speak:

> Can you drink the cup of submission? Yes, I realize full well what many of you are thinking: *That's all we've ever done.* But I would ask of you: Can you now drink the cup as Christ means you to drink it? Not because you must, but because you choose to? Would you be willing to put aside your legitimate rights, if the time to exercise them is not yet right in your particular circumstances? Would you be willing to put your career on hold, if that is in the best interests of your family or your cultural milieu? Will you work for change in a patient and loving manner; rather than sinking into anger or bitterness? Will you commit yourself to work in a Christ-like way, even if you are in un-Christ-like situations?[9]

So my activism as a Jesus feminist is marked and distinguished as being on behalf of others first.

My activism as a Jesus feminist is marked and distinguished as being on behalf of others first.

I rabble-rouse and disturb, advocate and make as much peace as I can, not for myself but for my son and daughters, and for other men and women, too—for their well-being, for their health, for their safety, for their happiness.[10]

That's the work of the gospel, isn't it? Not me first; it's you first—we're all equal to serve. I want both men and women to flourish in their God-ordained self; I want women around the world to be safe and well educated, to have rights of citizenship, voting, and property, safe arrivals of their babies, the choice of marriage for love, freedom from sexual exploitation. Our energy goes toward the Kingdom as part of our participation in Kingdom living, and we do it on behalf of others first.[11]

And remember, my friend—we do not labor in vain.

We are not like those who work and receive no harvest. Our harvest is coming, and it's bigger and grander than incremental goals approved by the UN, isn't it? We cling to the promise of God that injustice will not win and that Christ will set all things right, and we move a bit further into God's redemptive movement.

Do you mind if I stand here at the water's edge and cry at that very thought?

Oh, hallelujah.

Rest in it; hang onto it in the dark nights, when you're cold and alone here on the shore without a friend beside you and your pitiful sparking fire: he will make all things right. You do not labor in vain.

We love from the center of who we are.[12] And here is the beautiful thing about it all: as we rise up, stars in our eyes, prayer woven into our souls like smoke in our hair, we just might overturn the whole thing in the end, by the blood of the Lamb and the word of our testimony,[13] by the seed planted that grows to a mighty oak, by the yeast that causes the whole loaf of bread to rise, living prophetically and fully alive.

We do not grow weary in well doing.

We will see God's Kingdom come, here and now, outpost by outpost, home light by home light, a city on a hill for the weary travelers, a bonfire built on the sand for the ships still coming across the deep waters of love; it's our calling card.

But you are the ones chosen by God,
chosen for the high calling of priestly work,
chosen to be a holy people,
God's instruments to do his work and speak out for him,
to tell others of the night-and-day difference
he made for you—from nothing to something,
from rejected to accepted.

1 Peter 2:9 (MSG)

CHAPTER TWELVE

The Commissioning

Here, come and stand in front of me.

Stand on your own two feet; let's look each other right in the eye. It's a beautiful day dawning here at the water's edge. I picked a nice spot for us here, didn't I? The wind can take your breath, and your eyes are not satisfied with seeing at sunrise—I know.

Stand now, head up—you are loved, remember? You are loved, and you are free. There is no shame here.

Let me stretch my arms out wide, like an Old Testament prophet. My hands are a working mama's hands, a bit worn and lined. Let's do this properly.

Carry this with you; remember it, now:

I commission you.

In the mighty and powerful name of Jesus, I commission you for the work of the gospel as a minister of Jesus Christ, to live in your world as an ambassador of the Kingdom.

> **In the mighty and powerful name of Jesus, I commission you for the work of the gospel as a minister of Jesus Christ, to live in your world as an ambassador of the Kingdom.**

I commission you in the work of healing and serving and loving and reconciliation. You are an emissary of justice, and your work from now on is to put things right, to call those things that are not as they will be.

I pray that the God of hope would fill you with peace that passes all understanding. I pray that you will be drawn into community so rich, so deep, so diverse that you will disagree and fight and remain in fellowship together anyway. I pray that you will bring casseroles and prayer and laughter and tears to one another. I pray you would have your toes stepped on, your feelings hurt, and that you would forgive. I pray that you would be given the gift of realizing you were wrong about some important things. I pray that you would be quick to seek forgiveness and make it right when you are the transgressor.

Stop waiting for someone else to say that you count, that you matter, that you have worth, that you have a voice, a place, that you are called. Didn't you know, darling? The One who knit you together in your mother's womb is the one singing these words over you, you are chosen.

Stop waiting for someone else to validate your created self: that is done. Stop holding your breath, working to earn through your apologetics and memorized arguments, through your quietness, your submission, your home, your children, and your "correct" doctrine that God has *already* freely given to you.

Because, darling, you are valuable. You have worth, not because of your gender or your vocation or your marital status. Not because of your labels or your underlined approved-by-the-gatekeepers books or your accomplishments or your checked-off tick boxes next to the celebration you've mistaken as a job description in Proverbs 31.

In Christ, you have value beyond all of that. You abide in love; you can rest in your God-breathed worth. Can't you see? God has called you by name. He has written your name on the palms of his hands. You were knitted together; you are loved; you have been rescued already.

Now go. And do. You know Jesus—you have experienced the power and the grace with your own life; you have felt it in your own heart. Now go—heal, disciple, minister, love, loosen chains, throw open doors, bang your own pots and pans.

Speak, breathe, prophesy, get behind a pulpit and preach, mark exam papers, run a company or a nonprofit, clean your kitchen, put paint on a canvas, organize, rabble-rouse, find transcendence in the laundry pile while you pray in obscurity, deliver babies for Haitian mothers in the midwifery clinic—work the Love out and in and around you however God has made you and placed you to do it. Just do it. Don't let the lies fence you in or hold you back.

Love your spouse, love your babies, love the poor, love the orphans, love the widows, love the powerful, love the broken and the hurting, love your friends, love yourself, and love your enemies. Love until you come to love the whole world in the fullness of God, in the full expression of the image bearer he created you to be—just that; no more, but certainly no less.

Choose freedom. Choose the freedom of living loved, far from their debates and fence lines and name callings, and the belittling, divisive stereotypes. Extend the gift of freedom and grace, second chances, and more grace, just as you have received them. As E. E. Cummings wrote, it takes courage to grow up and turn out to be who you really are. Live counterculturally when the culture, baptized or secular, does not affirm truth, love, faith, mercy, and justice.

All of this matters, of course, because you matter, because your daughters and sons matter, because your sisters and brothers matter, because the people of God and the entirety of his created world matters, and the mission of God matters, because redemption matters. It matters whether you are silenced in Illinois or in India—whether it's your actual breathing life or your soul life—so we'll keep up the holy work, however that looks, keep prophesying with our very lives; we'll keep worshipping, keep loving, keep making space for God in the world and in each other, space for holy grace to fill. The Kingdom of God will be better with your voice, your hands, your experiences, your stories, your truth. You can go where I cannot go, and someone needs to hear you sing your song. You are someone's invitation.

Rest in your God-breathed worth. Stop holding your breath, hiding your gifts, ducking your head, dulling your roar, distracting your soul, stilling your hands, quieting your voice, and satiating your hunger with the lesser things of this world.

I pray for messy living rooms, for late nights, for dirty dishes littering your counters; and I pray for a faithful handful of friends and family to call when the darkness presses in close to you. I pray that you would be quick to show up at the right time for another person.

Come a little closer: I'm about to get all charismatic on you. Oh yes—I want to lay my hands right on your head. Let's do this.

I call you to joy, friend.

I set you apart in your right-now life for the daily work of liberation and love. Proclaim the Kingdom of God with your hands and your feet and your voice to every soul in your care and influence. May your soul long for prayer and for the Scriptures, may you keep secrets, may you give away your money, may you share your

> I set you apart in your right-now life for the daily work of liberation and love.

195

meals, and may you sit alone in silence outside under the sky and be satisfied. May you change the bedding in the middle of the night without anger after yet another childish accident, may you hold babies and comfort the dying and be the voice of knowledge tempered with grace and wisdom, and may you never forget how to sing and be silly. May you make room in your life to be inconvenienced and put out, and may you be Jesus with skin on for a few people. May you be fearless, and may you eat good food.

I pray that no matter your tool or method (mothering, preaching, cooking, writing, organizing, washing, teaching, building, money making—all of your whole life encompassing it all) you will walk in knowledge of the sacredness and purpose of your calling. I pray for dreams and visions, for the active leading of the Holy Spirit, and I pray you would never forget that Abba is very fond of you, and oh, what a friend you have in Jesus.

I pray for perseverance and for discipline; I pray for speech seasoned with salt.

I pray that when you are bored and tired and discouraged and frustrated, when you feel futile and small and ridiculous, you will never, never, never give up.

Your ministry, your work, begins now and it began long ago.

Turn around and face your life.

Look it in the eye, because this, right now—this is it.

If you are surrounded by jelly-faced toddlers or thousands of longing, hungry souls, or if you lift your head to find yourself in a hospital or a back alley or a church or an orphanage or your own suburban kitchen, if you are given a voice for dozens or only one other soul, you are a minister. Feel it; say the words; roll them against your teeth: you have been commissioned for the work of the gospel in Christ Jesus. You have. Keep your eyes open for the signs of God's presence; he's already at work in your world, revealing his ways to us all. You get to be a part of it, and I do, too.

We're in this together; let's do it together. We are calling people outside to the bonfire. There are a lot of us here, waiting for you in the open air. We've been here all along—don't you know? We've been ministering, preaching, praying, teaching, loving, mothering, caring, singing, walking each other home. It's glorious and messy, far away from the limitations, the barriers, and restrictive religion. But look, here—we, the people of God, are here with you; we are a family. We're your family, and we've been waiting for you.

Now I send you out.

I send you out to the spot where you are right now. You are right where you belong, you have everything you need to begin, and we will walk it out together. We are part of the redemptive movement of God in the world for his daughters and his sons. You and me—we are Kingdom people, an outpost of redemption, engaged in God's mission of reconciliation.

Blessed be his Kingdom, now and forevermore.

Peace be with you, my friend. Peace.

A Few Notes

I have made use of various translations and paraphrases of Scripture throughout the book. This was
done on purpose. Of particular note, although *The Message*
isn't a translation of the Bible (it's a paraphrase) and is not tra-
ditionally used for scholarly discussions, I made the choice to
use it in key passages of this book. First, clearly, this is not an
academic book. And second, I notice when Bible verses are
quoted or set apart in books, readers often skim through them
or skip right past, already convinced that they know what they
say because they've read them hundreds of times. My use of
The Message is deliberate: I want you to read these words, not

skip past them. And if I have to use a paraphrase to ensure the words aren't familiar to you, then I'm happy to endure the derision of scholars and purists for that choice.

Also, I have a lifelong habit of weaving memory verses, old songs, and hymns into my prose. This is often unintentional and unconscious on my part. However, I have made every effort to identify these phrases or ideas and give credit where it's due. If something sounds familiar to you, it's probably because it came from the Bible (in particular, I have a deep and abiding love for the Psalms and the book of Isaiah).

I have made the choice to change the names of many people involved in my story. My friends did not sign up to have their stories trotted out publicly, and I have made every effort to respect that wish or obscure a few details. The only exceptions are those cases of friends who already live a public life in some capacity either through speaking, ministry, leadership, blogging, or writing.

I also wish to clarify that I am not employed by any of the ministries or nonprofits mentioned here. (I did work for Mercy Ministries of Canada at one time.) Their inclusion in this book is because they are a significant part of my life. I do not speak for any of the leaders or ministries mentioned in any capacity. I have respected any confidentiality agreements. Any story or anecdote told here is prior public knowledge.

If you would like more information about any of these ministries, here are their websites:

A Few Notes

Mercy Ministries of Canada: www.mercyministries.ca

Mercy Ministries International: www.mercyministries.org

Help One Now: www.helponenow.org

The A21 Campaign: http://www.thea21campaign.org

Thank You

Thank you to my parents, David and Joan Styles, for loving Jesus with your whole hearts and loving each other, and your family, so beautifully. I've had a front-row seat for almost your entire marriage so I know the truth: you're the real deal. Thank you to my sister and lifelong-lobster, Amanda Slater, I love you to the moon and back, Mans. Thank you to my brother-by-marriage, Adam, and my two beautiful nieces, Addison and Ariana. Thank you to my Auntie, Donna Hobbs, for being one of the first women to teach me how to love without agenda or expectation of a return. Your legacy is more far-reaching than you will ever

know, I imagine. Thank you to Ed and Leona Bessey for raising such a mighty man of God and for spending your own
holidays looking after our tinies so that I could scribble in
coffee shops. Thank you to Leanna and Garin Johnston, to my
niece, Megan, and to Kim Kaszuba for their support. Thank
you to Sally and the entire Healy family, particularly Jared, for
being such a beautiful part of our family: I don't know who
loves you more, the tinies or me.

Thank you to the professors and students at Regent College in Vancouver, B.C., for wrecking our lives so beautifully.
Thank you to each of the diverse and disagreeing scholars,
theologians, writers, pastors, thinkers, and leaders whose
work influences and informs my own life.

Thank you to my motley collection of friends-like-family
all scattered across the world now, you're too many to name.
Thank you to my faith communities; in particular, Abbotsford
Vineyard, Relate Church's LifeWomen, Tree of Life Church,
and Regina Christian Centre. Thank you for your consistent
grace as I worked out these stories in our real lives before your
patient eyes, and thank you for now supporting and encouraging me in this new season. My experience with the Church
is restorative and beautiful because you have stuck with me.
Thank you to Susan and Josh Lepin for the use of your sacred space on Keats Island that one weekend. Thank you to
my secret P-Dubs—you know who you are. Thank you to my
readers and online community at www.sarahbessey.com; I
still can't believe anyone, other than my sister, actually reads

my rambling. You have all changed the trajectory of my life in many ways. Thank you to the *Deeper Story* community and also to the *SheLoves Magazine* global sisterhood. It's a privilege to be truth-telling and rabble-rousing with each of you.

Thank you to my soul sisters, Idelette McVicker, Tina Francis, and Kelley Nikondeha for your justice-seeking, Jesus-loving feminism, which inspires so much of my work and life. Thank you to my beloved sister-tribe for being gentle as doves and cunning as serpents, funny-as-hell, wise in counsel, and full of steadfast love: Nish Weiseth, Ashleigh Baker, Megan Tietz, Laura Tremaine, Arianne Segerman, Megan Cobb, Kelly Gordon, Amber Haines, Kelly Sauer, Missy Dollohan, Allison Ofelt, Kristin Potler, Chris Ann Brekhus, Leigh Kramer, Joy Bennett, Jen Johnson, and Emily Carter. Thank you to Rachel Held Evans for your guts, your wisdom, your generosity, your leadership, and your friendship.

Thank you to Pastor Helen Burns for your gracious leadership, your powerful voice, and your influence. Thank you to Mercy Ministries of Canada, in particular Nicola Bartel, for letting me be a small part of something so real and beautiful. Thank you to Nancy Alcorn for speaking in chapel back in 1997. Thank you to the Help One Now tribe, Chris Marlow, and Dan King. Thank you to the Haiti blogger team, particularly Jen Hatmaker, Kristen Howerton, Jennie Allen, and Mary DeMuth—so much of this is squarely your fault. Thank you to my new friends in Haiti: I want to stay and I want to listen.

Thank you to my literary agent, Rachelle Gardner, for her

wisdom, steady guidance, and encouragement. Thank you to my senior editor, Philis Boultinghouse, and to Nicci Hubert, Amanda Demastus, Carla Benton, and Kristin Roth, and the entire team at Howard Books.

Thank you to my heart's delight, Anne Styles, Joseph Arthur, and Evelynn Joan. I love being your Mumma-Bear, and I love our Five-Family, and I just plain like you. You changed everything for me.

Finally, always, thank you to my beloved husband, Brian Bessey. You are in every word of this book and every breath I take. I love living deliberately with you. Thank you for turning on the AM radio in that old Chevy, and then slow dancing at the side of the road with me on those starlit Tulsa nights so long ago. Thank you for "growing old with me, the best is yet to be." MTB.

And Jesus: if I had an alabaster box full of expensive perfume, I would smash it on my front sidewalk. I just want to be with you, walking in your way, always.

Discussion Questions

Chapter One: Jesus Made a Feminist Out of Me

- The title of this book comes with some big feelings for all of us. What feelings does "Jesus feminism" bring up for you initially?

- What women in scripture do you identify with most? How does (or might) Jesus interact with them?

- Does it seem radical to you that God believes women are people, too?

Chapter Two: A Redemptive Movement

- What ways do you see God—through the church or justice organizations—"moving us forward" toward a better understanding of his purpose?

Chapter Three: Tangled-Up Roots

- How did your parents' stories or family history impact your understanding of God and your place in the kingdom?

- Can you think of a woman in your childhood who stood out as "using her gifting," maybe even in spite of the laws or traditions of the church?

- Think about how gender differences were framed for you as a child or as a new believer. What stands out to you looking back? What do you understand as truth today?

- Have you ever had big questions you didn't feel your church wanted to hear or help you answer? How have you wrestled with those questions?

Chapter Four: The Silent(?) Women of Paul

- Sarah defines theology as simply "what we think about God and then living that truth out in our right-now life."

How do you understand and wrestle with theology in your own life?

- What baggage shows up on your emotional doorstep when you read scriptures about submission in marriage and to men? Does the context of Paul's writings to early Christians help you grapple with those issues?

Chapter Five: Dancing Warriors

- How do you interpret the Bible's call for mutual submission in marriage? Could you walk out the dance of "none but Jesus" in your home?

- Have you ever felt like a warrior alongside men in the Kingdom of God? If so, tell that story! If not, try on the armor—how does it feel?

Chapter Six: Patron Saints, Spiritual Midwives, and "Biblical" Womanhood

- What women—from Sarah's list or your own—stand out as "saints" and midwives in your spiritual journey?

- Where do you seek out and find women to shepherd you continually today?

- How can you embrace who God says you are—and walk in freedom from the law?

Chapter Seven: A Narrative Reborn

- Do you have an "and then everything changed" story—or maybe more than one?

- How do you understand the metaphor of birth and pregnancy connected to the story of God?

- What stories are you aching to tell that might testify to your unique experience with God?

Chapter Eight: Reclaiming the Church Ladies

- If you're completing these questions with a group of women, give yourselves exactly five minutes to share hilarious and horrendous stories from your personal women's ministry woes. (After five minutes, wipe the tears of laughter from your face, and let's build something new together.)

- What does authentic community between among women look like to you? Have you ever seen it done right in the church?

- What might it look like to de-segregate ministry in the church?

Chapter Nine: Moving Mountains One Stone at a Time

- Have you ever felt "the frequency of your heartbeat move to a new wavelength?" Revisit your miracle stories.

- How do miracles—big and small—change your view of God? Of yourself?

- What can you say YES to, with and for God?

Chapter Ten: Kingdom Come

- What do you imagine when you think of the Kingdom of God?

- How can you take part in the redemptive movement of God for women around the world? What hurt are you drawn to heal in even the smallest way?

Chapter Eleven: Intimate Insurgency

- What big questions come up for you as you go forward from here in your own life, church, and family?

- How can Jesus feminism embrace the "others first" spirit of the gospel?

- Does "Jesus feminism" mean something else to you now than it did when you picked up this book?

Chapter Twelve: The Commissioning

- What does it feel like to read Sarah's Commission?

- What words seem written just for your heart to hear?

Further Reading

If you would like to dive more deeply into the theology behind the ideas I've written through here, I've included this alphabetical list. Keep in mind that this is only the beginning of a vast field of scholarship and theology awaiting you.

Barton, Sara Gaston. *A Woman Called: Piecing Together the Ministry Puzzle*. Abilene, TX: Leafwood, 2012.

Beach, Nancy. *Gifted to Lead: The Art of Leading As a Woman in the Church*. Grand Rapids, MI: Zondervan, 2008.

Bosch, David Jacobus. *Transforming Mission: Paradigm Shifts in Theology of Mission*. Maryknoll, NY: Orbis Books, 1991.

Cunningham, Loren, and David Joel Hamilton, with Janice Rogers. *Why Not Women? A Biblical Study of Women in Missions, Ministry, and Leadership*. Seattle: YWAM Publishing, 2000.

Evans, Rachel Held. *A Year of Biblical Womanhood: How a Liberated Woman Found Herself Sitting on Her Roof, Covering Her Head, and Calling Her Husband Master*. Nashville: Thomas Nelson, 2012.

Escobar, Kathy. *Down We Go: Living into the Wild Ways of Jesus*. San Jose, CA: Civitas Press, 2011.

Grenz, Stanley J. *Theology for the Community of God*. Grand Rapids, MI: Wm. B. Eerdmans, 2000.

Grenz, Stanley J., with Denise Muir Kjesbo. *Women in the Church: A Biblical Theology of Women in Ministry*. Downers Grove, IL: IVP Academic, 1995.

Guder, Darrell L., ed. *Missional Church: A Vision for the Sending of the Church in North America*. Grand Rapids, MI: Wm. B. Eerdmans, 1998.

James, Carolyn Custis. *Half the Church: Recapturing God's Global Vision for Women*. Grand Rapids, MI: Zondervan, 2010.

Johnson, Alan F., ed. *How I Changed My Mind about Women in Leadership: Compelling Stories from Prominent Evangelicals* (featuring essays from Stuart and Jill Briscoe, John Ortberg, Tony Campolo, Bill and Lynne Hybels, and many others). Grand Rapids, MI: Zondervan, 2010.

Kristof, Nicholas, and Sheryl WuDunn. *Half the Sky: Turning Oppression into Opportunity for Women Worldwide*. New York: Alfred A. Knopf, 2010.

Kroeger Richard Clark, and Catherine Clark Kroeger. *I Suffer Not a Woman: Rethinking 1 Timothy 2:11-15 in Light of Ancient Evidence*. Ada, MI: Baker Academic, 1998.

Manning, Brennan. *The Ragamuffin Gospel: Good News for the Bedraggled, Beat-up, and Burnt Out*. Colorado Springs: Multnomah, 2005.

McKnight, Scot. *The Blue Parakeet: Rethinking How You Read the Bible*. Grand Rapids, MI: Zondervan, 2008.

———. *Junia Is Not Alone* (e-book). Englewood, CO: Patheos Press, 2011.

Newsom, Carol A., and Sharon H. Ringe, and Jacqueline E. Lapsley. *Women's Bible Commentary*. Louisville, KY: Westminster John Knox Press, 2012.

Saxton, Jo. *More Than Enchanting: Breaking Through Barriers to Influence Your World*. Westmount, IL: InterVarsity Press. 2012.

Scanzoni, Letha Dawson, and Nancy A. Hardesty. *All We're Meant to Be: Biblical Feminism for Today*. Grand Rapids, MI: Wm. B. Eerdmans, 1992.

SheLoves Magazine: Stories of the Sisterhood. www.shelovesmagazine.com.

Stackhouse, John G., Jr. *Finally Feminist: A Pragmatic Christian Understanding of Gender: Why Both Sides Are Wrong—and Right*. Ada, MI: Baker Academic, 2005.

Stevens, R. Paul. *The Other Six Days: Vocation, Work, and Ministry in Biblical Perspective*. Grand Rapids, MI: Wm. B. Eerdmans, 2005.

Sumner, Sarah. *Men and Women in the Church: Building Consensus on Christian Leadership*. Westmount, IL: Intervarsity Press, 2003.

Van Gelder, Craig. *The Essence of the Church: A Community Created by the Spirit*. Ada, MI: Baker Books, 2000.

Webb, William J. *Slaves, Women & Homosexuals: Exploring the Hermeneutics of Cultural Analysis*. Downers Grove, IL: InterVarsity Press: 2001.

Willard, Dallas. *The Divine Conspiracy: Rediscovering Our Hidden Life in God*. New York: HarperCollins, 1997.

Notes

Let Us Be Women Who Love

1. Idelette McVicker, "Let Us Be Women Who Love."
    SheLoves Magazine, originally published at http://
    shelovesmagazine.com/manifesto/, used with
    permission.

Introduction: A Bonfire on the Shore

1. Leonard Cohen, "Anthem," from the album *The
    Future,* (Columbia Records, 1992.)

Chapter One: Jesus Made a Feminist Out of Me

1.   John G. Stackhouse Jr., *Finally Feminist: A Pragmatic Christian Understanding of Gender: Why Both Sides Are Wrong—and Right* (Ada, MI: Baker Academic, 2005), 85.

2.   One example is Feminists for Life: http://www.feministsforlife.org.

3.   Stackhouse, *Finally Feminist*, 86.

4.   Ibid, 17.

5.   Carolyn Custis James, *Half the Church: Recapturing God's Global Vision for Women* (Grand Rapids, MI: Zondervan, 2010), 154.

6.   The phrase "through a glass, darkly" is from 1 Corinthians 13:12 (King James Version).

7.   Loren Cunningham and David Joel Hamilton, with Janice Rogers, *Why Not Women? A Biblical Study of Women in Missions, Ministry, and Leadership* (Seattle: YWAM Publishing, 2000), 111.

8.   Rachel Held Evans, *A Year of Biblical Womanhood: How a Liberated Woman Found Herself Sitting on Her Roof, Covering Her Head, and Calling Her Husband "Master"* (Nashville: Thomas Nelson, 2012), 72.

9.   Luke 1:46–55.

10.   See Galatians 3:28 and Colossians 3:11.

11.   John 8:3–11 (NLT).

12. The story of the woman with the issue of blood is found in three of the Gospels: Matthew 9:18–26, Mark 5:25–34, and Luke 8:43–48.

13. Luke 13:16.

14. Luke 13:16 (NLT).

15. Luke 10:42 (NLT).

16. John 11:25

17. John 11:25 (NLT).

18. John 4:7–30

19. Luke 11:27–28

20. Cunningham and Hamilton, *Why Not Women?*, 125.

21. Luke 8:3

22. John 20:17 (NLT). John 20:1 and Mark 16:9 identify Mary Magdalene specifically. Matthew 28:1 and Luke 24:1–10 identify the presence of others.

Chapter Two: A Redemptive Movement

1. Stackhouse, *Finally Feminist*, 39.

2. Romans 8:22

3. Seminary people call it the redemptive movement hermeneutic. I read more about it in William J. Webb's groundbreaking *Slaves, Women & Homosexuals: Exploring the Hermeneutics of Cultural Analysis* (Downers Grove, IL: InterVarsity Press, 2001). My first task when I heard this term, I admit, was to figure out what *"hermeneutic"*

meant, so for anyone else who is wondering, for our conversations, it's an explanation or interpretation that leads to a way of living.

4. In Matthew 5, Jesus delivers the Sermon on the Mount. In addition to the Beatitudes, Jesus teaches about the fulfillment of the law found in his life. He teaches about adultery, divorce, murder, and revenge, among other sins, with the phrase "But I tell you . . ." The example I've cited is near the end of the chapter in verses 38–48.

5. One example: Leviticus 25:44–46.

6. Colossians 4:1.

7. The book of Philemon is a letter from Paul to his brother in Christ, Philemon, encouraging him to accept a runaway slave, Onesimus, now that he has come to faith in Christ and wishes to return to his master.

8. For example, Ephesians 6:5 and Titus 2:9–10.

9. You can learn more about the A21 Campaign online at http://www.thea21campaign.org.

Chapter Three: Tangled-Up Roots

1. *Bullfrogs and Butterflies: God Is My Friend* (Burlington, VT: Birdwing Records), 1978.

2. Psalm 127:2

3. Isaiah 53:5

4. 2 Corinthians 6:14
5. Barbara Brown Taylor, *An Altar in the World: A Geography of Faith* (New York: HarperOne, 2010), 10.
6. All names connected with this part of our story have been changed out of respect and privacy.
7. Sara Miles, *Take This Bread: A Radical Conversion* (New York: Ballantine Books, 2005), 119.
8. Jonathan Martin. *Prototype: What Happens When You Discover You're More Like Jesus Than You Think?* (Carol Stream, IL: Tyndale, 2013), 50. Jonathan's entire book is wonderful, but the second chapter, *Beloved*, and the third chapter, *Obscurity*, gave me the gift of common language and camaraderie for this precious and difficult season of my life.
9. William Sears and Martha Sears, *The Birth Book: Everything You Need to Know to Have a Safe and Satisfying Birth* (New York: Little, Brown, 1994), 134.
10. Luke 6:44–45 (MSG)

Chapter Four: The Silent (?) Women of Paul

1. Genesis 32:24–29.
2. Evans, *A Year of Biblical Womanhood*, 294.
3. This method is called the Wesleyan Quadrilateral.

4. For an excellent discussion on this, check out the book I mentioned earlier: Rachel Held Evans' *A Year of Biblical Womanhood*, 74–95. My favorite quote: "We turned an anthem into an assignment, a poem into a job description" (89). Thanks to Rachel's book, I celebrate women in my own life with a rousing "Eshet chayil! "Woman of valor!"" now.

5. The phrase "half the church" is from Carolyn Custis James' book of the same title, *Half the Church*. This book is one of my own favorites, and James served as inspiration for certain portions of this book's scholarship, in particular the concept of the *ezer kenegdo*.

6. Matthew 9:36–38.

7. N. T. Wright, *Scripture and the Authority of God: How to Read the Bible Today* (New York: HarperOne, 2011).

8. Stackhouse, *Finally Feminist*, 23.

9. Galatians 3:28 (NLT).

10. Colossians 3:11 (NLT).

11. For clarification, this is because the Church was convinced of the imminent second coming of Christ.

12. Stackhouse, *Finally Feminist*, 51.

13. Cunningham and Hamilton, *Why Not Women?*, 192–193.

14. Ibid, 201.

15. 1 Corinthians 14:19 (NIV)
16. Cunningham and Hamilton, *Why Not Women?* 198–201.
17. Evans, *A Year of Biblical Womanhood*, 278.
18. Scot McKnight, *The Blue Parakeet: Rethinking How You Read the Bible* (Grand Rapids, MI: Zondervan, 2008), 202.
19. Cunningham and Hamilton, *Why Not Women?*, 214.
20. In fact, later in the letter (1 Timothy 4:1–5), and again in a future letter (2 Timothy 4:1–5), Paul cautioned against those false teachers in particular, so perhaps this section was also a connection point between how Eve was deceived and how we could all be deceived—not because of the weakness or inferiority of the gender, but because of a lack of wisdom.
21. Cunningham and Hamilton, *Why Not Women?*, 204.
22. Ibid, 203.

Chapter Five: Dancing Warriors

1. I'm showing my charismatic background with this phrase. "Jezebel spirit" is in reference to Queen Jezebel, wife of Israel's King Ahab. Jezebel appears in 1 and 2 Kings, as well as in Revelation. She was

the adversary of the prophet Elijah because she led the king and the nation of Israel into idol worship. In my memory, if a woman was accused of having a "Jezebel spirit," she was being accused of displaying characteristics or behaviors of manipulation, emasculation, domination, and control in the church or in her home. In more serious instances, an accuser was referencing Jezebel's practices of idol worship and sexual immorality, as well as her unrepentant sin. Unfortunately, this accusation gained popularity in the church for a time and has been wrongfully applied in some churches to all women who display leadership abilities, seem a bit "out of the box," or challenge authority in any way.

2. Carol A. Newsom and Sharon H. Ringe, *Women's Bible Commentary*, expanded ed. (Louisville, KY: Westminster John Knox Press, 1998), 463.

3. Celsus was a pagan critic who lived in the second century. This quote is from Ross Shepherd Kraemer's book, *Her Share of the Blessings: Women's Religions among Pagans, Jews, and Christians in the Greco-Roman World: Women's Religions among Pagans, Jews, and Christians in the Greco-Roman World* (Oxford: Oxford University Press, 1992), 128.

4. James, *Half the Church*, 111.

5. Evans, *A Year of Biblical Womanhood*, 207.

6. Victor P. Hamilton. *The Book of Genesis: Chapters*

1–17 (New International Commentary on the Old Testament) (Grand Rapids, MI: Wm. B. Eerdmans Publishing Company, 1990), 181.

7. The references are Genesis 2:18, 20; Isaiah 30:5; Ezekiel 12:14; Daniel 11:34; Exodus 18:4; Deuteronomy 33:7, 26, 29; Psalms 20:2, 33:20, 70:5, 89:19, 115:9–11, 121:1–2, 124:8, 146:5; and Hosea 13:9. These references are courtesy of James, *Half the Church*, 112.

8. J. R. Daniel Kirk, "Imaging the Biblical God," *Storied Theology* (blog) Theological God," February 2, 2012, http://www.jrdkirk.com/2012/02/02/imaging-the-biblical-god/.

9. James, *Half the Church*, 115.

10. Philippians 2:5–8 (NIV).

11. See Matthew 18:1.

12. See Mark 10:44.

13. Theologians such as Jürgen Moltmann, C. Baxter Kruger, and Miroslav Volf have developed the theology of perichoresis for today's generation.

14. Philippians 2:3–9.

15. Please know that my words about mutual submission are referencing an ideal conceptually, within the context of a healthy, life-giving marriage. If you or someone you know is suffering from abuse in any form, please seek real and substantial help after securing your safety.

Chapter Six: Patron Saints, Spiritual Midwives, and Biblical Womenhood

1. Selina Alko, *Every-Day Dress-Up* (New York: Knopf Books for Young Readers, 2011).
2. Eve's story appears in the early pages of Genesis, including Genesis 3.
3. Deborah's story appears in Judges 4 and 5.
4. Evans, *A Year of Biblical Womanhood*, 19.
5. Priscilla is mentioned in Acts 18, Romans 16, 1 Corinthians 16, and 2 Timothy 4.
6. P. J. Achtemeier, *HarperCollins Bible Dictionary*, rev. ed. (New York: HarperCollins, 1996), 882.
7. Anna the Prophetess is found in Luke 2:36–40.
8. Lydia is mentioned in Acts 16.
9. See 1 Corinthians 1:11
10. Romans 16:12.
11. See Philippians 4:2–3.
12. See Acts 21:8–9.
13. Romans 16:7.
14. James, *Half the Church*, 103.
15. Isaiah 30:21.
16. 1 Corinthians 13:4–7 (MSG).

Chapter Seven: A Narrative Reborn

1. The phrase "living loved" is borrowed with great appreciation from the work of Wayne Jacobsen of Lifestream Ministries.[Per official website] His book, *He Loves Me! Learning to Live in the Father's Affection* (Windblown Media, 2007), was a tremendous blessing to me at a crossroads time in my faith formation.

2. D&C is shorthand for dilation and curettage, a surgical procedure to scrape the interior of a woman's uterus and dispose of its contents. It can be an abortion procedure, but a D&C is also used to dispose of excess tissue in the uterus or, as was proposed in my case, to remove a miscarried baby from the womb in lieu of naturally occurring labor and delivery.

3. From a popular quote, usually attributed to Elizabeth Stone: "Making the decision to have a child—it is momentous. It is to decide forever to have your heart go walking around outside your body."

4. *The Book of Common Prayer and Administration of the Sacraments and Other Rites and Ceremonies of the Church: Together with the Psalter Or Psalms of David According to the Use of the Episcopal Church,* (New York: Church Publishing, 1979), 71.

5. The phrase "relax into this relationship" is inspired by Wayne Jacobsen's oft-used phrase "reality you relax into" in regards to living loved in Christ. For instance, it is used in his teaching series "Transitions" found here: http://www.lifestream .org/transitions. (Newbury Park, CA: LifeStream Ministries, 2009).

6. See 2 Timothy 2:13 (NIV)

7. Romans 8:15–17 (MSG).

8. Romans 8:18–28 (excerpt; MSG).

Chapter Eight: Reclaiming the Church Ladies

1. Living Hope centers are a project within Watoto in Uganda. You can learn more by visiting them online at http://www.watoto.com/returntodignity/living -hope/.

2. Vinson Synan. From an article called "Women in Ministry: A History of Women's Roles in the Pentecostal and Charismatic Movements" published in *Ministries Today*, January/February 1993, 46, http://www.regent.edu/acad/schdiv/assets/women _in_ministry.pdf.

3. Helen Rappaport. *Encyclopedia of Women Social Reformers* (Santa Barbara, CA: ABC-CLIO: 2001), 102.

4. J. Herbert Kane. Life and Work on the Mission Field (Baker: 1990), 143.

5. *Why Not Women?* 68.

Chapter Nine: Moving Mountains One Stone At a Time

1. I have changed the names of the Mercy graduates mentioned in this book to ensure their ongoing privacy. However, these particular stories are already public knowledge, as the graduates referenced here do speak and write about their experiences openly and have given permission to the ministry to share their testimonies. Understandably, not all graduates make this same choice.

2. As referenced on the UNICEF website, Info by Country, Haiti Statistics. Orphans, children (aged 0–17) orphaned due to all causes, 2009, estimate (thousands): 440,000. http://www.unicef.org/infobycountry/haiti_statistics.html.

3. Isaiah 61:3 (NLT).

4. 2 Kings 4:1–7.

5. Barbara Kingsolver. *Animal Dreams* (New York: HarperCollins, 1991), 299.

6. Martin Luther King Jr. *Strength to Love* (Minneapolis: Fortress Press: 1977), 61.

7. You can learn more about Amahoro at http://www. amahoro-africa.org.

8. You can read these stories in *SheLoves* at www. shelovesmagazine.com.

9. Wm. Paul Young, *The Shack* (Newbury Park, CA: Windblown Media, 2007), 235.

10. 1 Corinthians 12:4.

11. 1 Corinthians 12:27.

Chapter Ten: Kingdom Come

1. David Jacobus Bosch, *Transforming Mission: Paradigm Shifts in Theology of Mission* (American Society of Missiology Series) (Maryknoll, NY: Orbis Books, 1991), 176.

2. Dallas Willard, interview by Andy Peck, May 2002, http://www.dwillard.org/articles/artview. asp?artID=92.

3. Darrell Guder, ed., *Missional Church: A Vision for the Sending of the Church in North America* (Grand Rapids, MI: Wm. B. Eerdmans, 1998), 92.

4. Craig Van Gelder, *The Essence of the Church: A Community Created by the Spirit* (Ada: Baker Books, 2000), 89.

5. R. Paul Stevens, *The Other Six Days: Vocation, Work, and Ministry in Biblical Perspective* (Grand Rapids, MI: Wm. B. Eerdmans, 2000), 193.

6. Bosch. *Transforming Mission*. 390.

7. James, *Half the Church*, 76.

8. Stevens, *The Other Six Days*, 204.

9. C. Hoekendijk, *Kirche und Volk in der deutschen Missionswissenschaft* (Munich: Chr. Kaiser Verlag, 1967), quoted in Bosch, *Transforming Mission*, 384.

10. James 1:17.

11. N. T. Wright. *Surprised by Hope: Rethinking Heaven, the Resurrection, and the Mission for the Church* (New York: HarperCollins, 2009), 293.

12. Guder, *Missional Church*, 91.

13. United Nations Children's Fund (UNICEF), *The State of the World's Children* (New York: UNICEF, 2009), 18–19, http://www.unicef.org/rightsite/sowc/pdfs/SOWC_Spec%20Ed_CRC_Main%20Report_EN_090409.pdf.

14. Half the Sky Movement, "Gender-Based Violence," accessed May 25, 2013, http://www.halftheskymovement.org/issues/gender-based-violence.

15. Ibid.

16. Half the Sky Movement, "Economic Empowerment," accessed May 7, 2013, http://www.halftheskymovement.org/issues/economic-empowerment.

17. Half the Sky Movement, "Education," accessed May

7, 2013, http://www.halftheskymovement.org/issues /education.

18. United States Department of Justice, National Institute of Justice. *Extent, Nature, and Consequences of Rape Victimization: Findings From the National Violence Against Women Survey.* (US Department of Justice, 2006), 7. Full study can be read here: https://www.ncjrs.gov/pdffiles1/nij /210346.pdf.

19. For a brief summary of the phenomenon of sexualized violence in fashion advertising, check out Jenna Sauers's article for *Jezebel*, published on June 11, 2012. (Warning: Highly disturbing images.) http://jezebel.com/5916650/fashions-ongoing-violence-against-women/.

20. Pamela Paul, *Pornified: How Pornography is Transforming Our Lives, Our Relationships, and Our Families* (New York: Times Books, 2010) This book is a heavily researched secular look at the effects of pornography and it's growing acceptability in our culture. High discretion warning for the content of this book.

21. This is in reference to the 2013 Steubenville, Ohio, rape case. For a summary of the crime, see Dan Wetzel, "Steubenville High School Football Players Found Guilty of Raping 16-year-old girl," *Yahoo! Sports*, March 17, 2013. http://sports.yahoo.com

/news/highschool—steubenville-high-school-football-players-found-guilty-of-raping-16-year-old-girl-164129528.html.

22.   While certainly not the only, or worst, example of an inappropriate comedian, this first-person account of a Daniel Tosh rape joke at the expense of a woman in the audience can be read here: "So a Girl Walks into a Comedy Club. . . ." *Cookies for Breakfast,* 2012, http://breakfastcookie.tumblr.com/post/26879625651/so-a-girl-walks-into-a-comedy-club.

23.   Amy Lepine Peterson wrote an incredible essay called "The F-Word: Why Feminism Is Not the Enemy" for Patheos' *Christ and Pop Culture* blog (February 20, 2013). In that essay, she wrote, "I'm a Christian. And until the day when the world automatically understands that to mean that I believe in the full humanity and personhood of both men and women, you can also call me a feminist." You can read the full essay at http://www.patheos.com/blogs/christandpopculture/2013/02/the-f-word-why-feminism-is-not-the-enemy/.

24.   David Holloway. *The Church of England: Where Is It Going?* (Eastbourne: Kingsway Publications, 1985), 22.

25.   James, *Half the Church,* 19, 76.

26.   Ibid, 162.

Chapter Eleven: Intimate Insurgency

1. James 1:5.
2. *Women's Words: The Columbia Book of Quotations by Women.* Ed. Mary Briggs (New York: Columbia University Press, 1996), 309.
3. Romans 12:1–3.
4. Wayne Jacobsen, "How Do I . . . ?" *BodyLife,* March 2010, http://www.lifestream.org/bodylife.php?blid=58.
5. Matthew 10:40–42 (excerpt; MSG).
6. Isaiah 58:3–9.
7. Luke 14:10–11 (excerpt; MSG).
8. Romans 15:1–6.
9. Gretchen Gaebelein Hull, *Equal to Serve: Women and Men Working Together Revealing the Gospel* (Ada, MI: Baker Book House, 1998), 241.
10. Philippians 2:3–4.
11. Stackhouse, *Finally Feminist,* 98.
12. Romans 12:9 (MSG).
13. Revelation 12:11 (NIV).

About the Author

S arah Bessey is a writer and an award-winning blogger at sarahbessey.com. *Jesus Feminist* is her first book. Sarah is an editor at *A Deeper Story* and a contributor at *SheLoves Magazine*. She is a happy-clappy Jesus lover, a joyful subversive, a voracious reader, and a social justice wannabe. She lives in Abbotsford, British Columbia, with her husband, Brian, and their three tinies: Anne, Joseph, and Evelynn.